D1591593

DETROIT STUDIES IN MUSIC BIBLIOGRAPHY

General Editor   **Bruno Nettl**   University of Illinois at Urbana-Champaign

THE EXTANT MUSIC OF

RODRIGO DE CEBALLOS AND ITS SOURCES

By Robert J. Snow

DETROIT STUDIES IN MUSIC BIBLIOGRAPHY   NUMBER FORTY-FOUR

Detroit   1980   Information Coordinators

Cover, end sheets, title page design from detail
of manuscript illustrated on pages 98-99
Book design and incidental artwork by Vincent Kibildis

181632

To

Dragan Plamenac

Distinguished Scholar, Revered Teacher, Esteemed Friend

Contents

Illustrations

Acknowledgments

I am deeply indebted to all of the many Spanish, Portuguese and Central American archivists,
librarians and maestros de capilla *who, during the past several years,*
permitted me to investigate and microfilm innumerable music manuscripts
and related materials committed to their charge.
Only their generosity in this regard made this monograph possible.

THE EXTANT MUSIC OF

RODRIGO DE CEBALLOS AND ITS SOURCES

Thematic Incipits   Illustrations   Four Motets

THE EXTANT MUSIC OF RODRIGO DE CEBALLOS AND ITS SOURCES

This study originally was presented as one of several papers delivered at a colloquium held at the University of Illinois on May 8, 1976, as part of the festivities celebrating the awarding of the honorary degree Doctor of Humane Letters to Dr. Dragan Plamenac in recognition of his outstanding contributions to the field of musicology.

RODRIGO DE CEBALLOS, a contemporary and personal friend of Francisco Guerrero, the greatest and most renowned Spanish composer of the reign of Philip II, also enjoyed widespread fame during his lifetime. This is evident from the tribute paid to him by Vicente Espinel in *La casa de la memoria,* one of the poems constituting this poet's *Diversas rimas* of 1591.[1] After praising Guerrero and Juan Navarro as "dos hombres de saber profundo, / Maestros mios, y de todo el mundo," Espinel names "el gran çavallos, cuyas obras / Dieron tal resplandor en toda España," as the first of several other musicians whom he wishes to honor for the greatness they achieved in the practice of their art.[2]

In spite of the importance of the role that Ceballos thus seems to have played in the musical life of sixteenth-century Spain, he and his music have been largely ignored by music historians. Almost all of the facts we have concerning him and his career have been discovered during the course of investigations into other facets of Spanish music history. The only two musicologists until now who have devoted any appreciable

---

[1] Madrid: Luis Sánchez. A modern edition with introductory notes by Dorothy Clotelle Clark was published by the Hispanic Institute in the United States (New York) in 1956. In this edition the passage in question begins on page 93.

[2] The other musicians to whom the poet paid tribute were the composers Rodrigo Ordóñez, Ginés [de] Boluda and Melchior Gálvez; the organists [Antonio de] Cabezón, [Gerónimo] Peraza and [Diego del] Castillo; the theorist [Francisco] Salinas; the singers Antolín and Martín de Herrera; and four female performers: Doña Francisca de Guzmán, Ana de Suazo, Agustina de Torres and Doña Isabel Coello, the first three of whom were singers and the fourth a vihuelist.

amount of time to searching specifically for information about his life have been Felipe Pedrell and Juan B. de Elústiza.[3]

One of the reasons for this neglect undoubtedly has been the assumption, held since Pedrell, that most of Ceballos's music either has been lost or is preserved only in a manuscript which is in such a deteriorated state that much of its contents cannot be transcribed.[4] An examination of numerous manuscripts preserved not only in Spain and Portugal but also in South, Central and North America reveals, however, that this is not so. Contrary to the musicological literature dealing with Ceballos, his preserved compositions number about eighty—the exact number depends upon how they are counted —rather than some twenty, and these are to be found in over forty sources rather than in a dozen or so.[5] But before enumerating these works and trying to ascertain what other compositions by him may still lie hidden among the many anonymously preserved items in sources of the sixteenth, seventeenth and eighteenth centuries, a review of the few facts known about his life will serve to place him in his proper historical context.

BIOGRAPHY

Ceballos seems to have been born sometime between 1525 and 1530 in or near Aracena, a small town some seventy miles northwest of Seville.[6] If this date is correct, he would have been an almost exact contemporary

---

[3] Felipe Pedrell, in the entry "Ceballos (Rodrigo de)" in his *Diccionario biográfico y bibliográfico de músicos y escritores de música* (Barcelona, 1894-97), was the first lexicographer to present specific biographical information, not all of it correct, about the composer. His entry on Rodrigo is immediately preceded by one on Francisco Ceballos, chapel-master at the cathedral of Burgos from 1535 until his death in 1571. In this entry Pedrell, following Hilarión Eslava in his *Breve memoria de la música religiosa en España* (Madrid, 1860) and in his *Lira sacro-hispana* (Madrid, 1869), stated that Rodrigo and Francisco perhaps were brothers and attributed to Francisco certain motets now known to be the work of Rodrigo. F.-J. Fetis, who also followed Eslava, made the same erroneous attributions in his entry on Francisco in both the 1862 and 1878 editions of his *Biographie universelle* (Paris). The biographical data on Rodrigo which Rafael Mitjana discovered during the course of his investigations into the life of Fernando de las Infantas, however, make it seem highly improbable that the two men were related; see Appendix II of Mitjana's *Don Fernando de las Infantas* (Madrid, 1918). It also should be noted that not a single liturgical work is attributed to Francisco in any known source and that all works ascribed simply to "Ceballos" can now be shown to be the work of Rodrigo.

Additional biographical information was uncovered by Juan B. de Elústiza during the preparation of his and Gonzalo Castrillo's *Antología musical* (Barcelona, 1933) and presented as part of the prefatory material of this collection. The only other data we have was discovered by José López Calo when he was preparing *La música en la Catedral de Granada en el siglo XVI,* 2 vols. (Granada, 1963).

The entry on Rodrigo de Ceballos in the *Diccionario de la música Labor* (Barcelona, 1954) contains no new biographical information nor does the treatment accorded him by Robert Stevenson in his *Spanish Cathedral Music in the Golden Age* (Berkeley and Los Angeles, 1961). Neither does the entry in the first supplementary volume of *Die Musik in Geschichte und Gegenwart,* hereinafter referred to as MGG (Kassel, 1973), which is remarkable only for the fact that two of the five bits of biographical information presented there are wrong.

[4] See Pedrell's entry in his *Diccionario;* perhaps this is why nothing further has been heard about the *Obras completas* of Ceballos which the Instituto Español de Musicología announced nearly thirty years ago as one of its proposed publications. See *Anuario musical* 3 (1948): 235.

[5] The list of works given in the most recent article dealing with Ceballos, that which appears in the first supplementary volume of MGG, includes, in addition to six of the seven secular works known to be by him, only two mass ordinaries and thirteen other items, one of which, *Virgo Dei genitrix,* is the *secunda pars* of a previously listed work, *Exaltata est,* whereas another, *Dicebat Jesus,* is a work by Guerrero. The article is rendered even less useful by the fact that not a single specific manuscript source for any of these works is cited; the author merely states that manuscripts containing works by Ceballos can be found in the archives of one or another of eleven Spanish churches.

[6] See Elústiza and Castrillo, *Antología,* p. lxxxv.

of Guerrero, whose birth occurred either in 1527 or 1528, and of Philip II, who was born in 1528. He probably began his musical training as a choirboy in one of the more important churches in or near Aracena and continued it while serving in the same capacity either at the cathedral of Huelva, a city of some importance almost directly south of his natal area or, much more likely, at one or another of the collegiate churches or at the cathedral in the equidistant but far more important city of Seville. If he did serve as a choirboy in Seville, he probably pursued his studies in composition under the cathedral chapelmaster, Pedro Fernández de Castilleja, a distinguished pedagogue who was the teacher of so many of the outstanding Spanish composers of the second half of the sixteenth century that Guerrero, in the autobiographical preface to his *Viage de Hierusalem,* could justly refer to him as "el maestro de los maestros de España."[7] It also is probable that if Ceballos pursued his early music studies in Seville it was at that time that his friendship with Guerrero was formed.

The earliest documented evidence of Ceballos's presence in Seville dates only from 1553. According to an entry made in the *Actas capitulares* on October 7 of that year, the cathedral canons heard on that date a report, probably made by Guerrero, recommending that new polyphonic choirbooks be prepared for the choir because the ones then in use were extremely old and the repertory they contained was very ancient and no longer being sung in other Spanish churches. The canons accepted the recommendation and agreed to commission the copying of two or three new books which were to contain the best masses then being sung in order to improve the quality of the music performed in the cathedral services. The copyist was to be "Rodrigo de Ceballos, an unemployed musician residing in the city and competent to do the work." In return for preparing the new books Ceballos was to receive his living expenses during the time he was copying them and to be reimbursed for the cost of the materials.[8] This capitular act also is the first of several pieces of evidence documenting the relationship between Ceballos and Guerrero and, from what one knows about Guerrero's lifelong concern for any one in financial distress, one suspects that his request for new choirbooks may have been prompted almost as much by his desire to assist an unemployed friend as it was by the cathedral choir's need for a newer repertory of masses.

Ceballos is next heard of in June of 1554 as one of six contenders for the chapelmastership at Málaga, a position which had become vacant at the death of Morales sometime between September 4 and October 7 of the preceding year. Guerrero had been selected by the cathedral chapter as Morales's successor in an open contest held in February of 1554 but had changed his mind about leaving Seville only a few days after his installation as chapelmaster at Málaga and the chapter was forced to hold another competition in June. Perhaps Ceballos presented himself as a contender at Guerrero's suggestion. In any case, the candidates were duly examined and one of the other contenders, Juan de Cepa, chapelmaster of the duchess of Calabria, was declared the chapter's first choice and Ceballos their second. After a delay of almost five months, caused by the new requirement to prove *limpieza de sangre* or purity of blood in order to hold a chapelmastership, Cepa was confirmed as chapelmaster.[9]

Ceballos returned to Seville and secured employment there as a singer in some church other than the cathedral, possibly the collegiate church of San Salvador. This we know from a letter written in January, 1556, by the treasurer of the cathedral of Córdoba who was then in Seville looking for singers for his church

[7] The popularity of this book, first published in Seville in 1596, was so great that it was reprinted several times during the following century but usually without the autobiographical material.

[8] Seville, *Actas capitulares,* 1553-54, fol. 74r.

[9] See Andrés Llordén, "Notas históricas del personal de la Catedral de Málaga," *Anuario musical* 16 (1961): 117-20.

and for a possible successor to Alonso de Vieras, the elderly and somewhat infirm chapelmaster at Córdoba. In his letter the treasurer recommended Ceballos to the Cordoban chapter and the composer soon was invited to Córdoba for a personal interview. On June 1 the chapter voted to hire him and he began his duties there as a tiplist and as assistant to Alonso de Vieras on June 10. Toward the end of that year he visited Seville in order to be ordained and upon his return to Córdoba shared the title of *maestro de capilla* with Vieras until the latter's retirement in May of 1557.[10]

The Cordoban *Actas capitulares* contain no further references to Ceballos other than the usual ones dealing with routine financial matters such as salary payments and the lease of a certain house to him. From this we can assume that he fulfilled his duties to the satisfaction of all, since in sixteenth-century Spain a cathedral chapter was quick to turn its attention to the music personnel whenever a conflict arose among the members of the choir or the chapelmaster was negligent in one or another of his duties.

Surprisingly, our only information about Ceballos's compositional activity at this time comes from an entry in the *Actas capitulares* of the cathedral in Málaga, where Juan de Cepa rather than Ceballos had been elected chapelmaster a few years earlier. This entry, dated June 12, 1560, records that the cathedral recently had received as a gift from Ceballos a choirbook containing works of his and that the chapter had voted to send him a letter of thanks and six ducats. Unfortunately, this entry does not specify the contents of the volume but it does suggest that the four years which Ceballos had by then spent in Córdoba had not been unproductive ones.[11]

Ceballos resigned his position in Córdoba on October 1, 1561, in order to become chapelmaster at the Capilla Real in Granada. The reason for his departure from Córdoba presumably was the desire to better himself professionally. The musical forces maintained by the Capilla Real, the tomb of Ferdinand and Isabel and of their daughter Juana and her husband, Philip I, seem to have been somewhat greater than those of the Cordoban cathedral and Granada itself certainly was a city of far greater importance at that time. That his departure from Córdoba was an amicable one is evident from the fact that he was invited there in 1563 and again in 1567, this time along with Guerrero, to serve as one of the judges in competitions held to choose chapelmasters for the cathedral.[12]

Nothing whatsoever is known about his activities as chapelmaster at the Capilla Real because the *Actas capitulares* covering the years of his service have been lost. All we know is that he was appointed *maestro* by a royal decree dated June 28, 1561, that another royal decree of November 30 of the same year reconfirmed his rights as chapelmaster and guaranteed his vote in the cathedral chapter over the objections of the canons, that still another royal decree confirming his rights was issued on January 29, 1572, and that he died sometime in 1581, not in 1591, as is stated in the first of the supplementary volumes of MGG, which contains the most recent article on Ceballos.[13]

A systematic search for further information about Ceballos's life and professional career probably will yield additional information. As yet, civil records in the various cities in which he worked have not been

---

[10] See Mitjana, *Infantas*, pp. 118-21.

[11] The entry is quoted in *Infantas*, p. 119. The volume was delivered by Gerónimo de Barrionuevo, probably a close friend of the composer who may well be identical with the Varrionuevo to whom one of the voice parts of Ceballos's setting of *Ojos hermosos* is attributed; see item no. 76 in the thematic list of Ceballos's works given below.

[12] See *Infantas*, pp. 121-22.

[13] See López Calo, *La música en la Catedral de Granada*, 2: 117.

examined and the archives of churches in Seville where he may have served as a singer still need to be explored. Nevertheless, the main outlines of his career now are known and consequently one can make a far more intelligent search for and study of his music than is possible in the case of many of his contemporaries.

ARCHIVAL REFERENCES TO MUSIC BY CEBALLOS

That Ceballos composed a considerable amount of music for those portions of the liturgy which normally received polyphonic treatment in Renaissance Spain is evident from an inventory made of the music books owned by the Capilla Real in Granada either in 1590 or 1592, about a decade after the composer's death.[14] Of the eighteen choirbooks and twelve sets of part books in this list, three of the former and one of the latter contained music exclusively by Ceballos and a second set of part books, a collection of motets by different composers, also contained items by him. The entries for these books read as follows: "Un libro de çavallos de misas y motetes con sus tablas," "Un libro de çavallos de favordones de visperas. Esta maltratado," "Un libro de misas de ferias en pergamino de çavallos," "cinco libros de çavallos de fabordones," and "seis libros de finot afforados en papel destraça."[15]

Evidence that the last-mentioned set of part books contained music not only by Dominique Phinot but also by Ceballos and other composers comes not from the inventory under consideration but from one made in 1610. This later inventory, which begins by listing in identical wording the same eighteen choir-books and eleven of the twelve sets of part books cited in the earlier one and which concludes with a list of the items acquired in the intervening years, has a number of marginal notes amplifying or otherwise modifying the descriptions of the older holdings. Thus, after the entry for the "seis libros de finot" appears an annotation which reads "son de ceballos y otros autores. falta uno."[16]

A third inventory of the music books at the Capilla Real, that of 1629, also should be mentioned not only because it reveals that the music of Ceballos was still in use there almost half a century after his death but also because it, too, contains a marginal note of interest. Except for two additional entries at the end, this inventory essentially is identical to that of 1610 but after the entry listing Ceballos's "favordones de visperas," described as "maltratado" in the earlier inventories, occur the words "hallose muy maltratado."[17] These words, of course, provide the clue to the fate not only of much of Ceballos's music but to that of a large number of his contemporaries. Because the music of the last half of the sixteenth and the first quarter of the seventeenth century continued to be sung in Spanish churches well into the twentieth century, the original sources containing it eventually wore out and were replaced by new manuscripts into which were copied only those items which then formed part of the repertory of a choir. And because the scribes who

---

[14] Two copies of this inventory (and of the following one from 1610) are preserved. One is to be found in the Archivo de Simancas in legajo no. 282, folios 372v-373r, of the *Inventario del Patronato ecclesiástico,* a series of registers documenting the periodic inspections made of royal chapels in the sixteenth, seventeenth and eighteenth centuries by agents sent from the court. This copy was published by Edmond Vander Straeten, *La musique aux Pays-Bas,* 8 vols. (Brussels, 1867-88), 8: 466. The other occurs on folios 203v-204r of the *Libro de visitas* preserved in the archives of the Capilla Real in Granada and has been published by López Calo in "El Archivo de música de la Capilla Real de Granada," *Anuario musical* 13 (1958): 103-28. The two copies are identical except for details of spelling and punctuation. Straeten states that it was drawn up in 1590 whereas López Calo gives 1592 as the date.

[15] These entries are cited from the copy of the inventory preserved in the *Libro de visitas* in the archives of the Capilla Real; see López Calo, "El Archivo," p. 122.

[16] See Straeten, *La musique,* 8: 467, and López Calo, "El Archivo," p. 122.

[17] See López Calo, "El Archivo," p. 122.

prepared these manuscripts often failed to add the names of the composers whose works they included, many of the compositions thereby saved from oblivion have been transmitted to us only anonymously.

Further evidence that Ceballos composed a substantial amount of music for both the Mass liturgy and Vespers comes from archival documents relating to the repertory of the choir of the cathedral of Toledo, the primatial church of Spain. An inventory completed at Toledo on August 13, 1580, for example, reveals that one of the twenty-one volumes containing the repertory of polyphonic music then being sung by the cathedral choir was a collection of Magnificat settings and motets by Ceballos.[18] And an entry made in the *Actas capitulares* on April 22, 1586, states that the cathedral's chapelmaster, Ginés de Boluda, and its copyist, Alonso de Morata, had purchased in the name of the chapter "two volumes of music by Rodrigo de Ceballos, who had been chapelmaster of the Capilla Real in Granada, from Fray Pedro Durán, an Augustinian residing in that city." One of these volumes contained masses and motets by Ceballos and other composers whereas the other book consisted of "salmos, imnos y magnificas del mismo Rodrigo de Çavallos."[19]

A similar if not identical collection of Vespers music by Ceballos also was in use in the chapel of Philip II at about the same time. This is evident from the inventory made in 1602 of the approximately two hundred music books which had belonged to the king's household at the time of his death. In this inventory the books are grouped into three categories, "Libros de canto del servicio de la capilla," "Libros que fueron de la Reyna Maria," and "Libros que tiene el maestro de la capilla," and the description of the fifteenth of those in the third category reads: "Otro libro de ymnos, de fabordon, de Manificas de Çavallos, cubierto de pergamino, con las harmas reales en la primera hoja."[20]

The inclusion of works by Ceballos in the repertory of the cathedral choir in Toledo and in that of the chapel of Philip II indicates that his music was highly regarded during the later years of his life and immediately following his death. That it continued to enjoy favor at court can be seen from the inventory made of the choirbooks which were in regular use in the chapel of Philip III in 1612. This list, given in a document dated November 12 of that year and entitled *Conocimiento de cargo de los libros de canto que se le entregan para servir de la dicha capilla,* includes among its thirty-eight entries a volume of Vespers music by Ceballos; perhaps this was the same volume as that listed in the inventory of 1602. How truly distinguished was the company in which this volume of music was to be found in 1612 can be seen from the names of the other composers who also were represented by at least one volume of their music: Morales,

---

[18] This inventory, completed some two months before the death of the Toledan chapelmaster Andrés de Torrentes, lists the volume of music by Ceballos as item 10; see Madrid, Biblioteca Nacional, Ms. 14047.

[19] The lengthy entry relative to this transaction is given in its entirety by Pedrell in his *Diccionario* under the heading "Durán (Fray Pedro)." Nothing is known of Pedro Durán other than that he was a "Fraile agustiniano en Granada, escribano y puntador de libros." It is possible that he was a close relative of that Gerónimo Durán de la Cueva, also of Granada, who probably studied composition with Ceballos there and who was chosen *maestro de capilla* at Córdoba in the contest held there in 1567, the judges being Ceballos and Guerrero. The only preserved music of this composer, who retained the post of chapelmaster at Córdoba until his death in 1614, was thought by Mitjana (*Infantas,* p. 115, n. 1) to be a mass ordinary for seven voices which he had discovered in the archives of the Cordoban cathedral in the second decade of this century. This work could not be located when the present writer visited the archives in 1974 but he had the good fortune to discover there a complete cycle of Vespers hymns by Durán de la Cueva. Many of these are preserved in two different versions and some in three and a comparison of the various versions reveals much about the compositional process of Spanish composers during the last quarter of the sixteenth century.

[20] This inventory has been published twice, first by Straeten, *La musique,* 8: 352-83, and then by Alfonso Andrés, "Libros de canto de la Capilla de Felipe II," *Música sacro-hispana* 10 (1917): 92-95, 109-11, 122-26, 154-57, 188-90. In Straeten the manuscript in question is mentioned on page 378 and in Andrés on page 155.

Guerrero, Rogier, Alfonso Lobo, Victoria, Palestrina, Lassus, Clemens non Papa, Cornelius Canis, Crequillon, Sermisy and la Hèle.[21]   As for the continued popularity of his music at the Capilla Real in Granada, this can be deduced not only from the previously mentioned inventory of 1629 but also from the fact that a large number of the compositions which appear anonymously in certain manuscripts copied there in the eighteenth century have now been identified as being his works, as will be seen below.

The only other presently known archival reference to music by Ceballos is that which comes from the *Actas capitulares* of the cathedral of Málaga. As was mentioned above, the chapter there voted on June 12, 1560, to send to Ceballos, then chapelmaster at Córdoba, a letter of thanks and six ducats for a volume of his music which he recently had sent to them.

Unfortunately, none of these archival references contains specific information about the contents of the manuscripts they mention and at first glance they seem to tell one only that Ceballos composed masses, motets, psalms, hymns and Magnificat settings. If, however, one interprets the information they contain in the light of what is known about the compositional output of his contemporaries in similar professional situations one can establish a hypothetical canon of his works. And when this hypothetical canon is compared with a list of those compositions of his which already have been discovered, it will offer valuable suggestions to the person seeking to identify additional works by him.

EXTANT WORKS

Motets. Several of the archival documents just cited mention motets by Ceballos. The earliest of these is the inventory made of the music books at the cathedral of Toledo in 1580 in which there is listed a volume of Magnificat settings and motets by him. The next is the 1586 entry in the capitular acts of the same church in which it is reported that two choirbooks, one with masses and motets by Ceballos and other composers, had been purchased from an Augustinian priest in Granada. The others are the various inventories made in 1590 and later of the books at the Capilla Real in which are listed, among the volumes with music by Ceballos, a choirbook containing masses and motets by him and a set of part books containing motets by him, Phinot and various unnamed composers. Neither the choirbook nor the set of part books once owned by the Capilla Real seems to be extant nor does the volume of Magnificat settings and motets mentioned in the Toledan inventory of 1580. The volume of masses and motets which the cathedral of Toledo purchased in 1586 from the Augustinian in Granada, however, seems to be identical with the manuscript preserved in that cathedral's Biblioteca Capitular under the siglum Mus. B. 7.[22]

This manuscript was first cited in musicological literature by Felipe Pedrell in the entry on Ceballos in his *Diccionario*. After giving a brief description of the manuscript, Pedrell noted that on the verso of the unnumbered sheet which serves as a flyleaf at the front of the book there is a statement to the effect that it contains all of the motets composed by Ceballos and three of his masses as well as motets by other composers. He also remarked that the paper was so corroded by the ink that not a single composition could be transcribed. The manuscript is, indeed, in a deplorable state of preservation and large areas have entirely disappeared from the center of many of the folios. It remains an important source for the works

---

[21] This document is preserved in the Archivo general de Palacio in Madrid, Seccion administrativa, Oficios de la Real Casa, guardajoyas, legajo 902: "Matheo Romero, maestro de canto de la capilla real, Conocimiento de cargo."

[22] For a description and inventory of this manuscript, see Felipe Rubio Piqueras, *Códices polifónicos toledanos* (Toledo, 1925), pp. 23-24.

of Ceballos, however, not only because a few of the works in it can be transcribed if one exercises patience but also because it enables one to establish a rather definitive list of the motets composed by him. This can be done, even though the folio which contained the index has been lost, because the scribe entered the name of the composer of each item at the top of one or the other of the folios constituting the openings on which the items begin.

Thirty-nine of the sixty-seven motets presently to be found in this manuscript are attributed to Ceballos and on the basis of the inscription on the verso of the flyleaf one might assume that these are all the motets he composed.[23] It is more probable, however, that he composed forty or forty-one. This is suggested by the fact that all of the folios preceding folio 6 have been lost. The first of these missing folios, probably six in number since most of the fascicles of the manuscript consist of three foldings, must have been unnumbered and its recto side undoubtedly contained an index since a very faint mirror image of part of this faded onto the verso of the preceding flyleaf and can still be seen there. The last of these lost folios undoubtedly was numbered 5 and contained the beginning of the superious and tenor parts of Ceballos's *Regina caeli* because the altus and bassus parts of this item begin on folio 6*r*. The remaining ten internal pages of this fascicle, folios [i]*v-5r,* surely contained music and the fact that folios 6*r* through 117*r* are devoted exclusively to motets by Ceballos suggests that the music on these now missing folios also was by him.

Eight of the twenty-two four-part motets by Ceballos which appear in the Toledo manuscript, as well as a five-part setting of a troped *Deo gratias* by him, have long been known to be preserved also in one or the other or both of two manuscripts almost contemporary with those cited in the archival documents mentioned above. Each of these manuscripts has a relationship with Seville rather than Granada and this suggests that those works of his which they contain were composed while he still was residing in Seville and hence are some of his earliest compositions.

The earlier of these two manuscripts was copied for the choir of the cathedral of Seville in about 1560 and is preserved in the Archivo Capitular of the cathedral as Ms. 1. The index indicates that originally it contained a total of thirty-one settings of motet texts, Marian antiphons and tropes of the *Deo gratias.* Twenty of the pieces were by one or another of four composers associated in some way with the cathedral of Seville whereas eleven were by one or another of three foreigners. Thus, Guerrero was represented by ten items, Ceballos by five, Morales by three, Pedro Fernández de Castilleja by two, Josquin by eight, Jachetus by two and Gombert by one. Again, the music of Ceballos was in distinguished company.[24]

The other manuscript was compiled primarily by a certain Diego Sánchez, who perhaps began it while serving as *maestro de los mozos* at the cathedral in Seville from early in 1597 to July 26, 1598. He seems to have completed it in 1616 in Valladolid, the seat of government during much of the reign of Philip III, and today it is preserved there at the *parroquia de Santiago* or parish church of St. James. In musicological literature it sometimes is referred to as the Diego Sánchez codex and at other times it is cited by the name

---

[23] At least one investigator has misinterpreted this inscription, which reads "Lo que contiene en este libro es Todos los motetes Que hiço Çevallos a 4 y a cinco Con tres Missas suyas I tambien otros motetes de otros maestros escogidos," and has concluded that forty-seven of the motets are by Ceballos. In the manuscript, however, twenty of the twenty-eight other motets are attributed to Santos de Aliseda and two to Jerónimo de Aliseda, both of whom worked at the cathedral in Granada, whereas three others are by Morales, one by Dominique Phinot, one by Pedro Guerrero and one by Francisco Guerrero.

[24] For a description and inventory of this manuscript, see Higini Anglés, "La música conservada en la Biblioteca Colombina y en la Catedral de Sevilla," *Anuario musical* 2 (1947): 31-32.

of the church where it is preserved. It contains over eighty compositions, the majority of which are the work of composers belonging to the Andalusian school of composition. Only one item by a non-Spaniard was included; this was the *Pater noster* of Adriano Willaert, which enjoyed great popularity in Spain.[25]

The eight four-part motets and the troped five-part *Deo gratias* by Ceballos which appear in these two manuscripts, along with one other four-part motet of his which is in a late seventeenth- or early eighteenth-century choirbook at El Escorial, have until now been the only works upon which musicologists, beginning with Eslava, have based their opinions of Ceballos's worth as a composer of liturgical polyphony because almost no other sacred works of his were thought to exist in transcribable form. During the summer of 1973, however, while working at the Capilla Real in Granada, I discovered that all seventeen of the five-part motets attributed to him in Toledo Ms. Mus. B. 7 and twenty of the twenty-two four-part ones attributed to him in the same Toledan source appear anonymously in a well-preserved manuscript copied at the Capilla Real about 1700.[26] Thus, since it has proved possible to transcribe the remaining two four-part motets in the Toledan manuscript, all thirty-nine of the motets which Ceballos is known to have written have been recovered.

Masses. Three different manuscripts mentioned in the various archival documents cited above are said to have contained masses by Ceballos. These are the volume of motets and masses purchased by the Toledo cathedral in 1586 and now identified as probably being Ms. Mus. B. 7 of the Toledan Biblioteca Capitular, and the volume of masses and motets and the volume of "misas de ferias" listed in all three of the inventories of the Capilla Real. Again, neither of the volumes which once belonged to the Capilla Real seems to be extant.

As yet no "misas de ferias," those unpretentious little masses consisting of but a very short Kyrie, Sanctus and Agnus Dei and intended primarily for use on ferial days in Advent and Lent and on Rogation days, have been found with an attribution to Ceballos. It is, of course, reasonable to believe that he, as did many other composers of the period, wrote at least one such mass because during the last quarter of the sixteenth century there were many days on which an ordinary of this kind would have been used. But the probability of finding a ferial mass by Ceballos is slight because relatively few of these masses have been preserved. The need for them decreased during the course of the seventeenth and eighteenth centuries as the sanctoral cycle encroached on Advent and Lent and feasts of the saints and votive Masses began to be celebrated with increasing frequency on the weekdays of these penitential seasons.

Three cyclic mass ordinaries by Ceballos have, however, been preserved and all three are to be found in Ms. Mus. B. 7 of the Biblioteca Capitular of the cathedral of Toledo. One of these, *Missa Veni Domine,* is based on a chant antiphon sung in Advent and as yet it has not been found in any other source. Fortunately it can be transcribed in its entirety despite the deteriorated state of the manuscript. Another is based on a motet by Morales, *Simile est regnum caelorum,* and it, too, can be transcribed. It does not seem to exist in any other Spanish or in any Portuguese source but can be found in one of the late sixteenth- or early

---

[25] About thirty percent of the items in the manuscript appear there anonymously, some because the scribe seems never to have entered the composer's name and others because the composer's name has been trimmed off. The remaining seventy percent are attributed to Morales, Navarro, Francisco Guerrero, Ceballos, Villalar, Montanos, Pedro Guerrero, Robledo, Alexo Martín, Anchieta and Willaert. For a description and an incomplete and by no means error-free inventory of the manuscript, see Elústiza and Castrillo, *Antologia,* pp. xix-xxiv.

[26] For a description and inventory of this manuscript, see López Calo, "El Archivo," pp. 109-10.

seventeenth-century manuscripts belonging to the cathedral of Guatemala City.[27]

The third of the cyclic masses in the Toledo manuscript is a *Missa sine nomine* based on melodic material of the composer's own devising. Portions of this mass cannot be transcribed from the Toledo manuscript but fortunately it enjoyed great popularity and is preserved, usually under the name *Missa tertii toni,* in a number of other sources dating from the late sixteenth through the eighteenth century. It is to be found, for example, in a choirbook in the Archivo Musical of the Iglesia Metropolitana de la Virgen del Pilar in Saragossa and in one at the cathedral in Huesca, as well as in two manuscripts at the cathedral of Avila. It also is to be found in three sources copied in Guatemala. One of these is the previously mentioned choirbook at the cathedral of Guatemala City which contains his *Missa Simile est regnum caelorum* and another is the so-called Jacaltenango manuscript, actually a collection of remnants from various sixteenth- and early seventeenth-century Guatemalan choirbooks.[28] The third is one of the several Guatemalan choirbooks recently acquired by the Lilly Library at Indiana University.[29] It also is reported to appear in a manuscript at the cathedral of Pamplona and may be preserved anonymously in a manuscript choirbook at the cathedral of Santiago de Compostela as well as in a choirbook which was copied at Toledo in 1696 but now is in Germany.[30] The popularity of this mass can be explained in part by the fact that in the seventeenth century it became fashionable to make collections of ordinaries which consisted of eight masses, each of which was in a different one of the eight modes. Because few cyclic masses were written in the third mode Ceballos's *Missa tertii toni* was a prime candidate for inclusion in these collections.

No other cyclic masses by Ceballos have as yet been identified but in all probability he composed several more. This is suggested by the fact that many of his contemporaries who were of equal stature as composers and who held similar professional positions are known to have composed from as few as six or seven ordinaries to as many as sixteen or so and by the fact that although the inscription on the flyleaf of Toledo Ms. Mus. B. 7 states that the motets by Ceballos which are found in it are all that he composed, it does not make a similar claim for the three masses by him which it contains.

The archival documents from all three of the ecclesiastical establishments mentioned above also provide evidence that Ceballos wrote much music for Vespers. The choir of the cathedral of Toledo acquired a volume of his "salmos, imnos y magnificas" in 1586 and a "libro de ymnos, de fabordon, de Manificas" by him was in use in the chapel of Philip II at the time of this king's death. And until at least 1629 the Capilla Real in Granada possessed "un libro de çavallos de favordones de visperas" and "cinco libros de çavallos de fabordones."

---

[27] For a description and inventory of these three manuscripts, see David Pujol, "Polifonía española desconocida conservada en el Archivo Capitular de la Catedral de Guatemala y de la Iglesia parroquial de Santa Eulalia de Jacaltenango," *Anuario musical* 20 (1965): 3-9. The mass in question appears on folios 133*v*-152*r* in the first of the three manuscripts described. Recently a fourth manuscript, still undescribed, was discovered in the cathedral archives.

[28] For information about the Jacaltenango manuscript, see Pujol, "Polifonía española desconocida," pp. 9-10.

[29] Some information concerning these manuscripts can be found in Robert Stevenson, *Renaissance and Baroque Musical Sources in the Americas* (Washington, 1970), pp. 55-62, but it must be used with caution. For more accurate but less detailed information given in conformity with the numberings the manuscripts now have in the Lilly Library, Bloomington, Indiana, see *Census-Catalogue of Manuscript Sources of Polyphonic Music, 1400-1550* (American Institute of Musicology, 1979), entries BloomL 1, 2, 3, 4, 5, 6, 7, 8, 9, 14 and 15. The mass in question appears in the third manuscript.

[30] I have not yet been able to verify the presence of a copy of this mass at Pamplona. At Santiago it may appear as the third of the eight anonymous masses in the choirbook listed as Ms. 3 in José López Calo, *Catálogo musical del archivo de la santa iglesia catedral de Santiago* (Cuenca, 1972), pp. 38-39. Concerning the manuscript copied at Toledo in 1696, see Gustav Adolf Trumpff, "Die Messen des Cristóbal de Morales," *Anuario musical* 8 (1953): 121, n. 150.

It is fortunate that the records from the first two of these establishments explicitly indicate that the choirbooks in question contained settings of all three of the principal kinds of texts from which the Office of Vespers is constructed—psalms, hymns and the Magnificat—since the descriptions of the Vespers books owned by the Capilla Real in Granada state only that they contained "fabordones." It is probable, however, that the contents of these books were identical with the contents of the Vespers books owned by the Toledan cathedral and the chapel of Philip II.[31]

Psalms. As yet only two Vespers psalms with an attribution to Ceballos have been found in a Spanish source. These are a setting of *Dixit Dominus* in tone 4 and a setting of *Lauda Jerusalem* in tone 8 and they occur in Ms. 4 at the cathedral of Segovia, an undated choirbook copied there perhaps about 1700.[32] These two works probably were introduced into the Segovian cathedral choir repertory late in the sixteenth or early in the seventeenth century, a period when many of the choirs of the cathedrals in cities situated somewhat north and west of Madrid were greatly influenced by the chapel of the king.

The second of the two psalm settings in the Segovia manuscript, *Lauda Jerusalem*, also is to be found, along with four others explicitly attributed to Ceballos, in Ms. 8 of the library of the palace of the Braganza family in Vila Viçosa, Portugal. The four other psalms in this late seventeenth-century manuscript are another setting of *Dixit Dominus,* this time in tone 1, a setting of *Confitebor tibi* in tone 7, one of *Laudate pueri* in tone 8, and one of *In convertendo Dominus* in tone 3.[33]

Only one other manuscript containing psalms expressly attributed to Ceballos is presently known. This is the so-called Gutierre Fernández Hidalgo codex, which was copied at the cathedral in Bogotá Colombia, in the late sixteenth century and is still preserved there.[34] Four of the five psalms by Ceballos

[31] In Spain the term "fabordon" had a much wider meaning than its Italian counterpart, "falsobordone," and customarily was used to designate not only simple homophonic formulas to which any psalm could be sung but the more elaborate through-composed settings as well.

[32] This manuscript, which has lost its title page and any flyleaves it once may have had, now consists of 123 folios numbered 1-121, 121[bis], 122. It originally contained twenty-three Vespers psalms, three settings of the short responsory *In manus tuas,* two settings of the canticle *Nunc dimittis,* twenty-one Vespers hymns and one *Regina caeli.* Two additional hymns were added at the end of the manuscript in the late eighteenth or early nineteenth century. Many of the items seem to have been entered anonymously but others obviously have lost their attributions to the trimmer's shears and now only fourteen of the works carry the name of their composer. The names remaining are those of Pedro Serrano (1), Guerrero (2), Ribera (1), Sebastián López de Velasco (1), Ceballos (2), Navarro (4), Darro (1), Boluda (1) and Robledo (1). Seven of the anonymous works have been identified as being by Guerrero and thirteen prove to be by Navarro.

[33] For a description and inventory of this manuscript, see Manuel Joaquim, *Vinte livros de música polifónica do Paço ducal de Vila Viçosa, catalogados, descritos e anotados* (Lisbon, 1953), pp. 89-94.

[34] For biographical information about Gutierre Fernández Hidalgo see Robert Stevenson, "Colonial Music in Colombia," *The Americas* 19 (1962): 122-24. For a list of this composer's works, see the same author's "The Bogotá Music Archive," *Journal of the American Musicological Society* 15 (1962): 300-302, and his *Renaissance and Baroque Musical Sources,* pp. 13-14. Also see the recent catalogue of the Bogotá music archives by José Ignacio Perdomo Escobar, *El Archivo musical de la Catedral de Bogotá* (Bogotá, 1976), pp. 707-11. The codex which bears the name of this important New World composer contains thirty-five works, the vast majority of which are by him, as can be seen from the list of the manuscript's contents given under the entry "Libros de coro. Gutierre Fernández Hidalgo" (pp. 726-27) of the just mentioned catalogue. In addition to Ceballos, who is represented by five Vespers psalms and a *Salve Regina,* the only other composers who presently are known to be represented in the manuscript are Guerrero, Victoria, Juan de Herrera and Joannes Medine. The identification of certain of the anonymous works, however, may result in the addition of two or three more names to this list. I am indebted to Prof. Gerard Béhague, University of Texas at Austin, for placing at my disposal his microfilms of this and other manuscripts in the Bogotá cathedral archives.

in this manuscript are settings of *Dixit Dominus*. The one in tone 1 is identical with the setting of this text in the Vila Viçosa manuscript and the one in tone 4 is the same as the *Dixit Dominus* in Segovia. The setting in tone 3, however, and the one in tone 6 occur nowhere else with an attribution to Ceballos but, as will be seen below, they do occur elsewhere anonymously. The fifth psalm is a setting of *Confitebor tibi* in tone 7 which, except for the music for verses 8 and 10, is identical to the setting in Vila Viçosa.

Among the manuscripts in which one or another of the eight psalms now known to be by Ceballos appears anonymously are two in Granada. The earlier of these is Ms. 4 of the Capilla Real. Copied in 1704, it contains among its twenty-four different settings of psalm texts Ceballos's *Dixit Dominus* in tones 4 and 6.[35] The other is Ms. 4 of the cathedral. This manuscript, which was copied in about 1735, contains thirty-three different settings of psalm texts. Four of these are by a mid-seventeenth-century cathedral chapelmaster named Gregorio Portero whereas the other twenty-nine are all anonymous and date from the late sixteenth century. Here, in addition to the two settings of *Dixit Dominus* by Ceballos which also appear in Ms. 4 of the Capilla Real, there occurs the setting of *Lauda Jerusalem* in tone 8 which is ascribed to him in the Segovia and Vila Viçosa manuscripts.

Two other manuscripts which contain several of Ceballos's psalms among their anonymous works are Libros de coro VI and XIX at the cathedral in Puebla, Mexico.[36] In the first of these one finds copies of all but two of the eight psalms mentioned above, *Confitebor tibi* and *Laudate pueri,* and in Libro XIX are to be found the setting of *Dixit Dominus* in tone 1 and *Confitebor tibi,* the latter of which is erroneously attributed to Guerrero. Consequently, the Puebla archives are the principal repository for psalms by Ceballos. This is explained, of course, by the fact that the cathedral of Puebla was established by and long remained dependent on the cathedral of Toledo.

Ceballos surely composed more than eight settings of psalm texts and in all probability several of the anonymously preserved psalms in the two Granada manuscripts just mentioned are his works. But before one can profitably speculate as to which these might be, one must determine which of them cannot be ascribed through concordance to one or another of his contemporaries. And this cannot yet be done since the work of sorting out the vast number of anonymously preserved works dating from the late sixteenth century has only begun.

Hymns. A situation similar to that encountered in the discussion of Ceballos's psalms also prevails for his hymns. Thus, only two Spanish manuscripts attribute hymns to him. One of these is Ms. 1 of the monastery of Guadalupe, an early seventeenth-century source which contains a setting of strophe 2 of the Epiphany hymn *Hostis Herodes impie;* a setting of strophe 4 of *Pange lingua,* for Corpus Christi; and a setting of strophe 2 of *Aurea luce,* sung on the Feast of Saints Peter and Paul.[37] The other source is Ms. 34 of the Archivo Musical of the Iglesia Metropolitana de la Virgen del Pilar in Saragossa. This is a tenor part book copied about 1650 and here, in the midst of a great variety of sacred and secular items, one finds superius I

---

[35] This manuscript is described and inventoried in López Calo, "El Archivo," pp. 110-12. The setting in tone 6 appears here twice.

[36] For a general description of the manuscripts at Puebla and a list of their contents, see Stevenson, *Renaissance and Baroque Musical Sources,* pp. 208-20.

[37] For a description and inventory of this manuscript and of Ms. 2 of the same archives, see David Crawford, "Two Choirbooks of Renaissance Polyphony at the Monasterio de nuesta Señora of Guadalupe," *Fontes artis musicae* 24 (1977): 145-74.

of strophe 4 of Ceballos's *Pange lingua.*[38] The hymns preserved in the Guadalupe manuscript probably entered the repertory of the choir there by way of the not-too-distant cathedral of Toledo, which exercised great influence on the liturgical and musical practices of this important religious house, but nothing can safely be conjectured as to the route by which the strophe in the Saragossa part book reached Aragon.

The principal source for hymns by Ceballos is the previously mentioned Portuguese manuscript from Vila Viçosa. Four of the hymns in this book are attributed to him—*Ave maris stella,* for Marian feasts; *Exsultet caelum laudibus,* for feasts of apostles and evangelists; *Pange lingua,* for Corpus Christi; and *Vexilla Regis,* for Passiontide—and each of them has a separate setting for each of the even-numbered strophes of its text.

The only New World source with a hymn expressly attributed to Ceballos is Libro de coro XIX of the cathedral of Puebla, which contains strophes 2 and 4 of his *Pange lingua.* Two other *libros de coro* at Puebla, however, contain his *Vexilla Regis* anonymously. These are numbers I and II.

The only other sources presently known to contain hymns by Ceballos are two manuscripts in Granada and in both of these the music appears not only anonymously but with texts other than those it has in the other sources containing it. Thus, the music used for strophe 2 of the Epiphany hymn *Hostis Herodes impie* appears in the previously mentioned Ms. 4 of the Capilla Real and in Ms. 5 of the cathedral of Granada with the text of strophe 2 of the hymn *Quicumque quaeritis,* for the Feast of the Transfiguration. And the music for strophe 2 of *Ave maris stella* in the Vila Viçosa manuscript appears in Ms. 5 of the Granada cathedral with the text of the fifth strophe of this hymn.

The six hymns by Ceballos which have so far been found probably constitute only about twenty percent of his work in this genre. This estimate is based on the assumption that in about 1575 he was obliged to compose a new cycle of Vespers hymns as a result of the introduction into Spain of the Breviary of Pius V. On many liturgical occasions the hymn texts which traditionally had been used at Vespers on the Iberian Peninsula differed from those in use in Italy and the Breviary of Pius V, one of the results of the liturgical reforms called for by the Council of Trent, was based on Italian usage. Consequently, when this Breviary was introduced into the various Spanish dioceses during the course of the decade or so following its publication in 1568, Spanish composers had to provide, with considerable haste, settings for a large number of hymn texts previously not used at Vespers in their country. It was primarily this situation, of course, and not, as sometimes has been assumed, a natural predilection on the part of Spanish composers for writing Vespers music rather than mass ordinaries, that prompted the creation of an unusually large number of collections of music for this service during the final decades of the Renaissance.

If Ceballos actually did compose a complete cycle of Vespers hymns according to the usage of the Breviary of Pius V, some twenty-two hymn settings by him still await discovery. The logical place to begin looking for

---

[38] This part book contains a single voice part, usually the tenor, of ninety-two items, the vast majority of which are motets. Thirty-six of these are by Juan Pérez, an important late Renaissance maestro de capilla at El Pilar, many of whose works are preserved completely but anonymously in other sources where they can be identified as the work of Pérez only through concordance with the tenors in this part book; Ms. 1 of the Archivo Capitular of the cathedral of Tarazona is one such manuscript. The majority of the other works are by Spanish composers such as Morales (17), Ribera (6), Navarro (5), Vicente (2), Ceballos (1), Corita (1), Josephus Gaz (1) and Pedro Guerrero (1). The non-Spaniards represented are Lasso (5), Ruffo (5), Palestrina (3), Clemens non Papa (2), de Monte (1), Fabricio de Entichi (1), Ferrabosco (1), Jachet (1), Mestre Jhan (1) and Petit Jan de Lambre (1). The one other item, *Sancta Trinitas, unus Deus,* is attributed to Morales here but in other sources to Craen, Festa, Fevin or Josquin.

these is, of course, Granada and a number of the hymns preserved anonymously in Ms. 4 of the Capilla Real and in Ms. 5 of the cathedral display stylistic and technical features remarkably like those of the hymns known to be by him. But, again, before attributing any of these to Ceballos it will be necessary to determine if any of them can be identified as the work of one or another of his contemporaries.

Magnificat Settings. Only a single Magnificat setting by Ceballos has yet been found in a Spanish source. Written in tone 2, it appears with an attribution to him in the Guadalupe manuscript which also contains three of his hymns and consists of all of the odd-numbered verses of the text. This leads one to assume, on the basis of Spanish practice in the latter half of the sixteenth century, that Ceballos composed a Magnificat cycle consisting of a series of eight settings of the odd-numbered verses of the text, one in each of the eight tones. And this assumption proves to be correct. Just such a cycle has been preserved and in it the setting in tone 2 is identical with the setting in the Guadalupe manuscript. This cycle occurs in whole or in part, and with attributions to Ceballos for all eight of its settings, in three different manuscripts at the cathedral of Bogotá, Colombia. Because none of these manuscripts has been assigned an archival siglum I shall refer to them here as Mss. A, B and C.

The youngest of the manuscripts, Ms. C, is the only one which is preserved in its entirety and is the only one in which the Magnificat cycle appears in its complete form. This manuscript was prepared in the late eighteenth or early nineteenth century and is a copy of a portion of Ms. A, the oldest of the three since it dates from about 1584. Ms. A is now in a badly deteriorated state and hardly more than half of its nearly two hundred original folios are still in existence. Fortunately, thirty of the thirty-six folios on which Ceballos's Magnificat cycle appeared are extant and a comparison of these with Ms. C reveals that the younger manuscript is a faithful copy of the older one. Ms. B probably was a copy of about the same portion of Ms. A as was Ms. C and seems to have been made about 1725. The paper used for it, however, was of very poor quality and only half a dozen or so of its folios still exist. A comparison of these with Ms. A suggests that it, too, was a faithful copy.[39]

Spanish Renaissance practice leads one to suspect that Ceballos also composed a second Magnificat cycle consisting of settings of the even-numbered verses of the text. And this suspicion is strengthened by the attribution to him of a setting in tone 6 of the even-numbered verses of this canticle in one of the Guatemala City manuscripts mentioned earlier.[40] As yet, however, no cycle containing the same setting has been found.

---

[39] For information about Ms. A in addition to what may be found in Stevenson's "Colonial Music in Colombia," "The Bogotá Music Archive" and *Renaissance and Baroque Musical Sources*, see *Census-Catalogue*, entry "BogC s.s." and Perdomo Escobar, *El Archivo musical*, entry "Libros de coro. Misas de Cristóbal de Morales" (pp. 727-28). Perdomo Escobar makes no mention in his catalogue of the fragments designated here as Ms. B but cites Ms. C in the entry "Ceballos, Rodrigo de. Magnificat omnitonum" (pp. 703-4). Here he also makes reference to two other Bogotá sources containing Vespers music by Ceballos. These are two sets of part books which were copied in 1762 and which contain, in addition to his Magnificat in tone 1, certain of his psalms which also appear in the Gutierre Fernández Hidalgo codex.

[40] See Pujol, "Polifonía española desconocida," p. 6. I have not yet been able to examine any of these Guatemala City manuscripts nor have I been able to acquire microfilms of them. Because of this, the inventory listing for this work, item no. 65, below, appears without incipits.

Other Liturgical Works. None of the archival records considered earlier mentions music by Ceballos for Compline but settings by him of the last two of the four psalms called for at this Office Hour in the Breviary of Pius V, Psalms 90 and 133, as well as of the canticle, the short responsory and the versicle sung at this service, are preserved in a Spanish manuscript copied in 1608 and now owned by the Hispanic Society of America.[41] In all probability he also provided settings for the first two psalms then sung at Compline, Psalms 4 and 30, but no trace of them has yet been found. The only other liturgical pieces presently known to be by him are the troped *Deo gratias* previously mentioned as being in Ms. 1 of the Archivo Capitular of the cathedral in Seville and a *Benedicamus Domino* in Ms. 1 of the monastery archives at Guadalupe.

Secular Works. Only seven secular pieces by Ceballos have as yet been located, six of them in the famous *cancionero* long known as Medinaceli Ms. 13230.[42] Two of those which appear in this manuscript do so anonymously, however, and have been identified as works by Ceballos only through concordance with intabulations in Estéban Daza's *El Parnasso,* which contains four works by this composer. The seventh item, *Pues ya las claras fuentes,* is known only in the instrumental version in which it appears in Daza's collection. The vocal versions of three of the six works by Ceballos in the Medinaceli manuscript, *Amargas oras, Duro mal, terrible llanto* and *Ojos hermosos,* are unique to this *cancionero* but the other three are to be found in one or both of two other manuscripts. Thus, *Quan bien aventurado* and *Rosales, mirtos, plátanos* are in Valladolid, Archivo Capitular, Ms. 17, and *Dime manso viento* is in the same manuscript and in Libro de coro XIX of the Puebla archives.[43]

These seven *canciones* surely constitute but a small portion of those which Ceballos wrote but it seems unlikely that a significant number of additional secular works by him will ever be identified even if they are extant because most of the preserved sixteenth- and early seventeenth-century *cancioneros* already have been studied in detail and published. Consequently, we must accept the fact that most of Ceballos's *canciones* are lost.

---

[41] A facsimile of folio 119r of this manuscript, which shows the beginning of the altus and bassus parts of the *Nunc dimittis,* appears on page 392 of [Clara Louisa Penney et al.], *A History of the Hispanic Society of America. Museum and Library. 1904-1954* (New York, 1954). In this publication the work is erroneously attributed to Morales and, on page 380, it is said to be for the Feast of the Purification. The manuscript was acquired by the Hispanic Society from the Leipzig antiquarian Karl W. Hiersemann, who offered it for sale at the end of the first decade of this century in his catalogue no. 380 entitled *Bibliotheca Iberica.* The items listed in this catalogue came primarily from the libraries of two deceased Spanish bibliophiles, one of whom was Federico Olmeda, *maestro de capilla* at the cathedral of Burgos for many years and a friend of Felipe Pedrell and his collaborator in the study of Spanish music history. That Olmeda acquainted Pedrell with this manuscript is evident from the copy of the two psalms, made in the original notation but not by Pedrell, preserved among Pedrell's papers at the Biblioteca Central in Barcelona as item no. 8 (pp. 17-36) of Ms. 787bis. See Higini Anglés, *Catàleg dels Manuscrits Musicals de la Col·leccio Pedrell* (Barcelona, 1921), p. 25.

[42] After the death of the previous duke the Medinaceli collection of music manuscripts and books, except for Ms. 607, was sold to Bartolomé March, of the famous Catalan family of industrialists and financiers. The collection now is housed at the home of Bartolomé March in Madrid but I cannot say whether it has been recatalogued and the items assigned new numbers or not. The present location of Ms. 607 is uncertain. It recently was offered for sale in the United States by a well-known antiquarian but was not identified as being the famous Medinaceli manuscript. I have been unable to ascertain if it is still in the hands of the antiquarian or has been sold. The most recent rumor is to the effect that it has been returned to Spain.

[43] For a description and inventory of this Valladolid manuscript, which is a tenor part book, see Higini Anglés, "El Archivo musical de la Catedral de Valladolid," *Anuario musical* 3 (1948): 83-86.

DUBIOUS AND LOST WORKS

One additional motet can tentatively be ascribed to Ceballos. This is *Gaude Dei genitrix,* which seems to be preserved only in Ms. 3 of the Capilla Real. Because thirty-seven of the thirty-nine works preserved in this source, all of them anonymously it will be remembered, prove to be by Ceballos on the basis of concordance with Toledo Ms. Mus. B. 7, one wonders if *Gaude Dei genitrix,* one of the two other motets, may have been the work which appeared in the now-missing first fascicle of the Toledo book. It is a rather long item which occupies four openings, folios 50*v*-54*r,* in Ms. 3 of the Capilla Real and could easily have been spread over the five openings formed by the ten internal pages, folios [i]*v*-5*r,* of the fascicle now missing from Toledo Ms. Mus. B. 7. Furthermore, its appearance here as the first item of the Toledo collection would have been in keeping with the general organizational plan of the book because the next twelve folios, 6*r*-17*r,* are occupied by four other Marian motets in the company of which *Gaude Dei genitrix* appears in Ms. 3 of the Capilla Real. Thus, since there is nothing of a stylistic nature in this motet that would preclude its being by Ceballos, one can assume that it very possibly is a work of his. A judgment more definitive than this should not be made until one has a greater degree of certainty that it cannot be identified by concordance as the work of another composer. It should be noted that the one other motet in Ms. 3 of the Capilla Real, *In illo tempore: Cum turba plurima,* is not by Ceballos; rather, it is a well-known work by Morales but it may well have been included in the manuscript on the erroneous assumption that it, too, had been written by Ceballos.

A set of nine *falsobordone* formulas for Vespers psalms also might be the work of Rodrigo de Ceballos. The evidence for this comes solely from Volume VI of Felipe Pedrell's *Hispaniae schola musica sacra,* where, on pages 20-22, he published eight of the formulas with an attribution simply to "Ceballos," the only attribution they had in the unspecified manuscript from which they were transcribed. This can be seen from the prefatory notes to these items, on pages xiv and xvi of the same volume, where Pedrell described them as a "colección transcrita de un libro de atril de la cual hay copias en diversas catedrales," and considered the question of whether they were written by Francisco or Rodrigo without resolving the problem. Unfortunately, it is still not known what manuscript it was that served as the source for Pedrell's edition.[44]

Mitjana, in his study of Spanish music in Lavignac's *Encyclopédie de la musique,* also mentioned these formulas and stated that he had seen a copy of them "conservé dans un livre de choeur de la Cathédrale de Malagá." From the context in which he speaks of them it is obvious that he considered them to be the work of Rodrigo.[45] None of the formulas is to be found in any manuscript book presently in the archives of the cathedral of Málaga, however, and one suspects that the "livre" to which Mitjana referred was the appropriate volume of Pedrell's *Hispaniae schola musica sacra.* This suspicion is strengthened by the fact that all of the notational and musical details of the formula for tone 3, which Mitjana provided as an example of Ceballos's work, agree completely with those in the edition of this tone as it was presented by Pedrell.

The recent discovery of these formulas in a manuscript obviously not the one on which Pedrell's edition was based does not help resolve the question of authorship. This early seventeenth-century source, which

---

[44] A late nineteenth-century copy of these formulas in their original notation was found among Pedrell's papers after his death and they now constitute item no. 1 (pp. 1-12) of Ms. 788*bis* in the Biblioteca Central in Barcelona; see Anglés, *Catàleg,* p. 33. These items are not in Pedrell's handwriting and one thus suspects that they were sent to him by his friend Federico Olmeda, who sent him copies of a number of works in their original notation, often without complete bibliographic information. Consequently, Pedrell himself may never have known from which manuscript they were copied.

[45] *Premiere Partie. Histoire de la musique. Espagne-Portugal* (Paris, 1920), p. 1975.

consists of forty-one folios, is preserved in the library of the abbey of Montserrat as Ms. 750 and is one of several relatively unknown choirbooks there with exclusively Spanish material.[46] All of the folios through 36*r* contain music primarily for Holy Week but folios 36*v*-41*r* have the same eight *falsobordone* formulas which Pedrell printed plus one in tone 5, which he does not seem to have known. (The final tone in both Pedrell's edition and in Ms. 750 is designated *octavus irregular*, which today usually is called *tonus peregrinus*.) No composer is indicated either in the index or in the body of this book but a superscription on folio 37*r* does tell one that the formulas were used at the royal monastery at El Escorial: *Como se cantan en s. lorencio. Pueden yr por qualquier psalmo y son muy acomodados.* A similar statement occurs in the index. Thus, all that one can as yet say about the authorship of these formulas is that, if they were indeed attributed to "Ceballos" in a late sixteenth-or early seventeenth-century manuscript known to Pedrell but now lost or destroyed, Rodrigo de Ceballos rather than Francisco is more likely to have been the composer because all other works with an attribution simply to "Ceballos" have been proved to be the work of Rodrigo.

Pedrell also is the source of information about a lost set of the *Lamentationes* of Jeremiah. In the entry on Ceballos in his *Diccionario* he lists twelve pieces by the composer which he said were preserved in an incomplete set of part books then owned by a friend of his, the violinist and composer Jesús de Monasterio.[47] Eleven of these works are motets which also are preserved in Toledo Ms. Mus. B. 7 and in Ms. 3 of the Capilla Real. The textual incipit of the twelfth, however, is *Et factum est postquam in captivitatem* and this is the opening of the line which in Spain was used to introduce the singing of the *Lamentationes* at Matins on Holy Thursday until the use of the Breviary of Pius V became mandatory. Unfortunately, the Monasterio part books are now lost if not destroyed, and because Pedrell provided no thematic incipits it is impossible to say if one of the anonymously preserved settings of the *Lamentationes* which antedate the introduction of the Breviary of Pius V is by Ceballos.

Other works by Ceballos may well be found as musicologists continue their explorations in cathedral archives on the Iberian Peninsula and in Central and South America and more sources for the works presently known undoubtedly will be discovered. Enough of his music is now available, however, to make it possible to affirm that he was indeed one of the most important composers of the reign of Philip II. More than this cannot be said until more is known about the music of his contemporaries.

---

[46] The presence of these formulas in Ms. 750 was brought to my attention by a former student of mine, Carl Manns, who worked in the library at Montserrat late in 1978. The other manuscripts there with music exclusively by Spanish Renaissance composers are those numbered 751, 752, 753, 754, 774, 775 and 1085. See the recently published catalogue of this library: Alexandre Olivar, *Catàleg dels manuscrits de la Biblioteca del Monestir de Montserrat* (Monestir de Montserrat, 1977).

[47] For information concerning Monasterio, see José Subirá, "Epistolario de Fr. A. Gevaert y J. de Monasterio," *Anuario musical* 16 (1961): 217-46.

THE EXTANT MUSIC OF

RODRIGO DE CEBALLOS
AND ITS SOURCES
Thematic Incipits   Illustrations   Four Motets

THEMATIC INCIPITS OF THE EXTANT WORKS

SIGLA FOR ORIGINAL SOURCES

AvilaC 1   Avila. Catedral, Archivo Capitular. Ms. 1.

AvilaC 2   Avila. Catedral, Archivo Capitular. Ms. 2.

BloomL 3   Bloomington. Indiana University, Lilly Library. Latin American Manuscripts, Guatemala. Music Ms. 3.

BogC A   Bogotá. Catedral, Archivo Musical. Incompletely preserved manuscript without number copied *c.* 1584-86.

BogC Apost   Bogotá. Catedral, Archivo Musical. Set of five part books copied in 1762 containing music for Vespers of Apostles.

BogC B   Bogotá. Catedral, Archivo Musical. Fragments of seven consecutive folios from a manuscript copied *c.* 1725.

BogC C   Bogotá. Catedral, Archivo Musical. Manuscript without number copied *c.* 1800.

BogC GFH   Bogotá. Catedral, Archivo Musical. Gutierre Fernández Hidalgo Codex.

BogC Virg   Bogotá. Catedral, Archivo Musical. Set of five part books copied in 1762 containing music for Vespers of Virgins.

Daza	Daza, Estéban. *Libro de música en cifras para vihuela intitulado el Parnasso.* Córdoba: Diego Fernández, 1576.
EscSL 2	El Escorial. Real Monasterio de San Lorenzo de El Escorial, Biblioteca y Archivo de Música. Ms. 2 (*olim* 4).
EscSL 4	El Escorial. Real Monasterio de San Lorenzo de El Escorial, Biblioteca y Archivo de Música. Ms. 4 (*olim* 2).
EscSL 7	El Escorial. Real Monasterio de San Lorenzo de El Escorial, Biblioteca y Archivo de Música. Ms. 7 (*olim* 8).
GranC 3	Granada. Catedral, Archivo Capitular. Ms. 3.
GranC 4	Granada. Catedral, Archivo Capitular. Ms. 4.
GranC 5	Granada. Catedral, Archivo Capitular. Ms. 5.
GranC LN	Granada. Catedral, Archivo Capitular. Set of six part books designated as *Libros negros.*
GranCR 3	Granada. Capilla Real, Archivo Capitular. Ms. 3.
GranCR 4	Granada. Capilla Real, Archivo Capitular. Ms. 4.
GranCR 6	Granada. Capilla Real, Archivo Capitular. Ms. 6 (a set of four part books).
GuadM 1	Guadalupe. Real Monasterio de Santa María, Archivo. Ms. 1 (=A=I).
GuatC 1	Guatemala City. Catedral, Archivo Capitular. Ms. 1.
GuatC 2	Guatemala City. Catedral, Archivo Capitular. Ms. 2.
HuescaC 52	Huesca. Catedral, Archivo Capitular. Ms. 52.
JacalP 7	Jacaltenango. Iglesia Parroquial de Santa Eulalia, Archivo Musical. Ms. 7.
JaenC s.s.	Jaen. Catedral, Archivo Capitular. Paper manuscript of 102 folios without number.
MadBM 13230	Madrid. Biblioteca Medinaceli. Ms. 13230 (see note 42, above).
Monasterio PB	Three part books (S, A, T) once owned by Jesús de Monasterio which now are lost or destroyed.
MontsB 750	Montserrat. Monestir de Montserrat, Biblioteca. Ms. 750.
NYorkHS 380/870	New York City. The Hispanic Society of America, Library. Ms. 380/870.
PampC	Pamplona. Catedral, Archivo Capitular. Unspecified manuscript reported to contain Ceballos's *Missa tertii toni.*
PuebC I	Puebla. Catedral, Archivo Musical. Libro de coro I.
PuebC II	Puebla. Catedral, Archivo Musical. Libro de coro II.
PuebC VI	Puebla. Catedral, Archivo Musical. Libro de coro VI.
PuebC XIX	Puebla. Catedral, Archivo Musical. Libro de coro XIX.

SantiC 3	Santiago de Compostela. Catedral, Archivo Capitular. Ms. 3.
SaraP 8	Saragossa. Iglesia Metropolitana de la Virgen del Pilar, Archivo Musical. Ms. 8.
SaraP 34	Saragossa. Iglesia Metropolitana de la Virgen del Pilar, Archivo Musical. Ms. 34 (tenor part book).
SegC 4	Segovia. Catedral, Archivo Capitular. Ms. 4.
SevCA 1	Seville. Catedral, Archivo Capitular. Mus. Ms. 1.
Tol 1696	Manuscript copied in Toledo in 1696 and now in an undisclosed location in Germany; see note 30, above.
TolC 7	Toledo. Catedral, Archivo y Biblioteca Capitulares. Ms. Mus. B. 7.
VallaC 17	Valladolid. Catedral, Archivo de Música. Ms. 17 (tenor part book).
VallaP s.s.	Valladolid. Parroquia de Santiago. Manuscript without number copied by Diego Sánchez.
VilViçB 8	Vila Viçosa. Casa de Braganza, Museu-Biblioteca. Ms. 8.

SIGLA FOR MODERN PUBLICATIONS

Araiz	Araiz Martínez, Andrés. *Historia de la música religiosa en España.* Barcelona, 1942.
Elústiza	Elústiza, Juan B. and Gonzalo Castrillo Hernández, eds. *Antología musical.* Barcelona, 1933.
Eslava	Eslava, Hilarión, ed. *Lira sacro-hispana.* 10 vols. Madrid, 1869.
López	López Calo, José. *La música en la Catedral de Granada en el siglo XVI.* 2 vols. Granada, 1963.
Morphy	Morphy, Guillermo, ed. *Les Luthistes espagnols du XVIᵉ siècle.* Leipzig, 1902.
Pedrell	Pedrell, Felipe, ed. *Hispaniae schola musica sacra.* 8 vols. Barcelona, 1894-98.
Penney	[Penney, Clara Louisa et al.] *A History of the Hispanic Society of America. Museum and Library. 1904-1954.* New York, 1954.
Perdomo	Perdomo Escobar, José Ignacio. *El Archivo musical de la Catedral de Bogotá.* Bogotá, 1976.
Querol	Querol Gavaldá, Miguel, ed. *Cancionero musical de la Casa de Medinaceli.* 2 vols. (Monumentos de la música Española, Vols. VIII-IX.) Barcelona, 1949-50.
Rubio	Rubio, Samuel, ed. *Antología polifónica sacra.* 2 vols. Madrid, 1954-56.
Trend	Trend, John Brande. *The Music of Spanish History to 1600.* Oxford, 1926.

MOTETS a 4

1. *Adversum me susurrabant omnes*

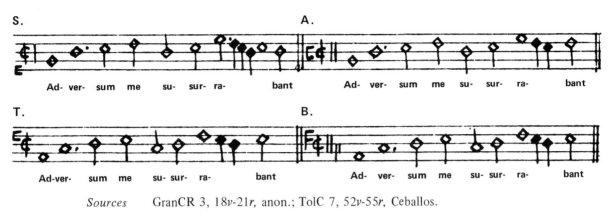

Sources   GranCR 3, 18*v*-21*r*, anon.; TolC 7, 52*v*-55*r*, Ceballos.

Modern Edition   Number 2 of Four Motets, pages 136-42.

2. *Ascendens Christus*

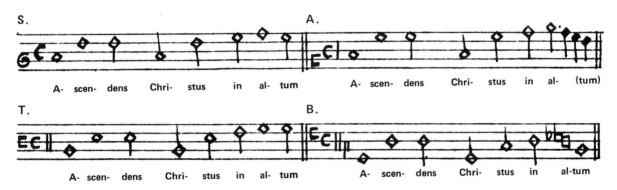

Secunda pars

Sources   GranCR 3, 54*v*-60*r*, anon.; TolC 7, 26*v*-31*r*, Ceballos.

3. *Clamabat autem mulier*

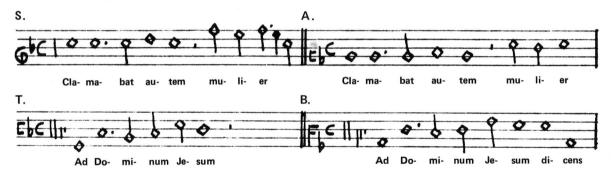

Sources	GranCR 3, 8*v*-10*r*, anon., *Dominica 2.ª [in Quadragesima];* Monasterio PB, Ceballos; TolC 7, 43*v*-46*r*, Ceballos.
Modern Edition	Number 1 of Four Motets, pages 131-35.

4. *Cum accepisset Jesus panes*

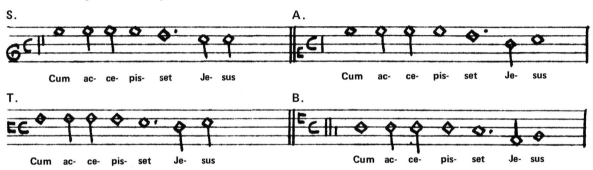

Sources	GranCR 3, 12*v*-14*r*, anon., *Dominica 4.ª [in Quadragesima];* Monasterio PB, Ceballos; TolC 7, 48*v*-50*r*, Ceballos.

5. *Ductus est Jesus in desertum*

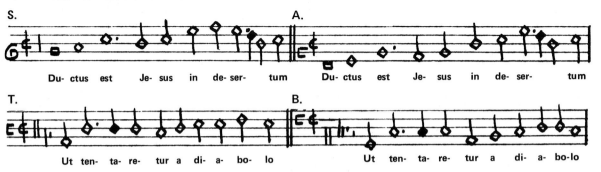

Sources	GranCR 3, 6*v*-8*r*, anon., *Dominica I in Quadragesima;* Monasterio PB, Ceballos; TolC 7, 40*v*-43*r*, Ceballos; VallaP s.s., 32*v*-33*r*, Rodrigo çaballos, *dominica prima in quadragesima.*
Illustration	Folios 6*v*-7*r* of GranCR 3, Illustration 1, pages 84-85.

6. *Ecce sacerdos magnus . . . et in tempore*

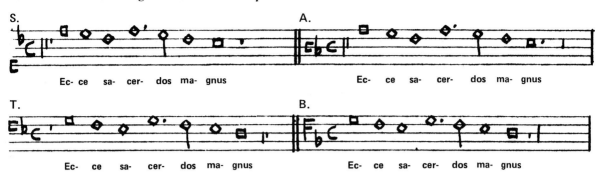

Sources   GranC LN, No. 23, anon.; GranCR 3, 65*v*-67*r*, anon.; TolC 7, 19*v*-21*r*, Ceballos.

7. *Ego quasi vitis fructificavi*

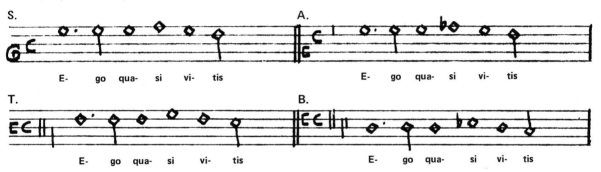

Sources   GranCR 3, 48*v*-50*r*, anon.; Monasterio PB, Ceballos; SevCA 1, 91*v*-93*r*, Roderice cevallos; TolC 7, 7*v*-9*r*, Ceballos.

8. *Erat Jesus ejiciens daemonium*

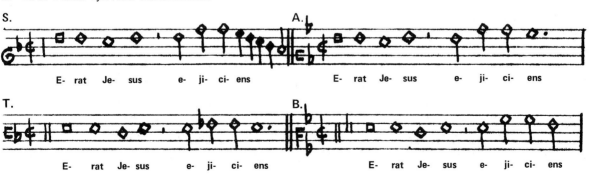

Sources   GranCR 3, 10*v*-12*r*, anon., *Dominica 3ª [in Quadragesima]*; TolC 7, 46*v*-48*r*, Ceballos; VallaP s.s., 33*v*-34*r*, Rodrigo çaballos, *in dominica 3 XL.*

Modern Edition   Elústiza, pages 154-56.

Illustration   Folios 33*v*-34*r* of VallaP s.s., Illustration 2, pages 86-87.

9. Eripe me, Domine

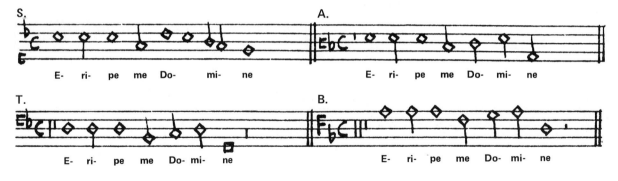

Secunda pars

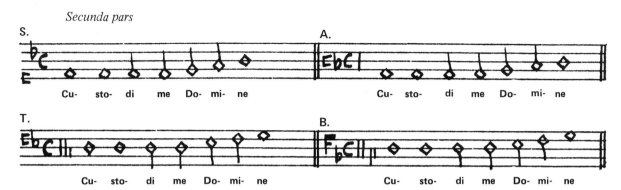

Tertia pars

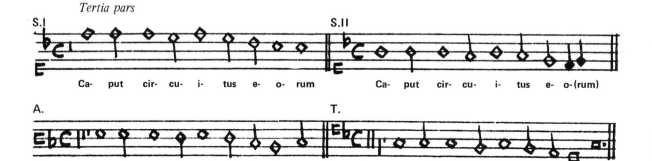

Quarta pars

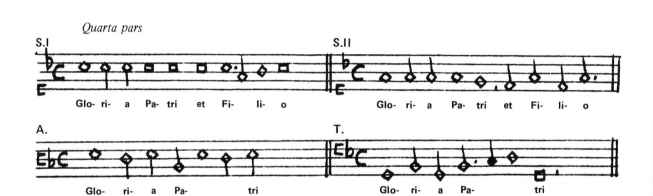

Sources   GranCR 3, 21*v*-31*r*, anon.; TolC 7, *prima pars:* 50*v*-52*r*, *secunda and tertia partes:* 34*v*-38*r*, *quarta pars:* lacking, Ceballos.

10. *Erravi sicut ovis*

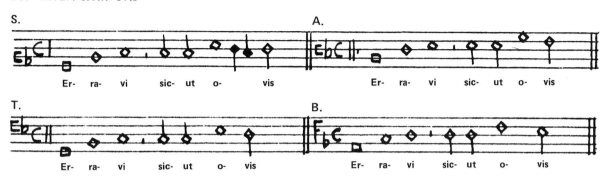

Sources   GranCR 3, 16*v*-18*r*, anon.; TolC 7, 55*v*-57*r*, Ceballos.

11. *Exaltata est*

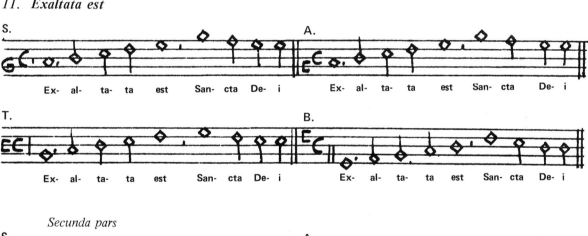

Secunda pars

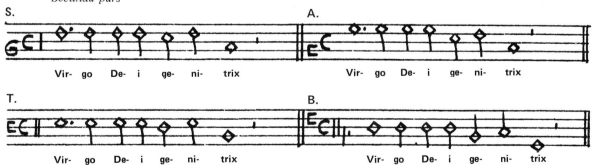

Sources   GranC 3, 48*v*-50*r*, anon., *secunda pars* only; GranCR 3, 44*v*-48*r*, anon.; Monasterio PB, Ceballos; TolC 7, 13*v*-17*r*, Ceballos; SevCA 1, 93*v*-95*r*, Roderice cevallos.

Modern Edition   López II: 136-39, *secunda pars* only.

12. *Exaudiat Dominus*

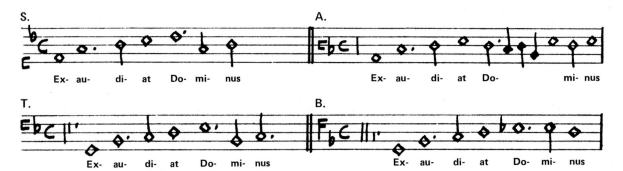

Sources	EscSL 2, 58*v*-59*r*, Zaballos; GranCR 3, 34*v*-36*r*, anon.; GranCR 6, No. 11, anon.; TolC 7, 57*v*-59*r*, Ceballos.
Modern Edition	Eslava I-1: 106-8 (attributed to Francisco Ceballos).

13. *Haec dies*

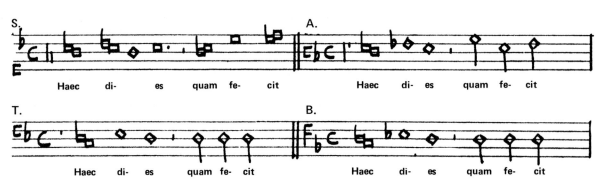

Sources	TolC 7, 205*v*-206*r*, Ceballos.

14. *Hortus conclusus*

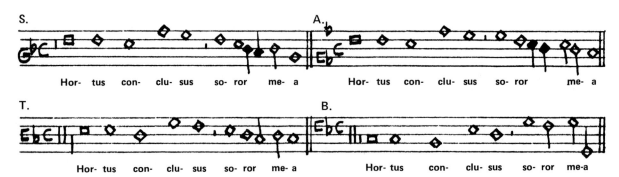

Secunda pars

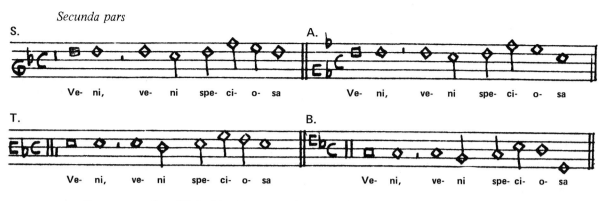

Sources   GranCR 3, 39*v*-44*r,* anon.; Monasterio PB, Ceballos; SevCA 1, 87*v*-91*r,* Roderice cevallos; TolC 7, 9*v*-13*r,* Ceballos; VallaP s.s., 54*v*-56*r,* R⁰ çaballos.

Modern Edition   Elústiza, pages 144-50; Eslava I-1: 96-101 (attributed to Francisco Ceballos).

15. *Inter vestibulum*

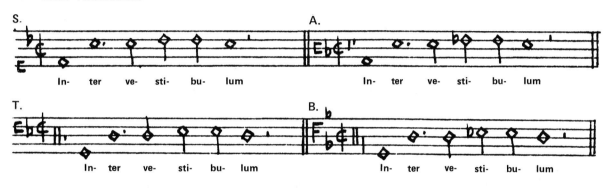

Sources   EscSL 4, 61*v*-62*r,* Zaballos; EscSL 7, 52*v*-53*r,* Zaballos; GranCR 3, 1*v*-3*r,* anon., *Fer. ij. Hebdom. j. Quadrag.;* TolC 7, 38*v*-40*r,* Ceballos; VallaP s.s., 31*v*-32*r,* Rodrigo çaballos, *in feria quarta çinerum.*

Modern Edition   Araiz, pages 266-72 (attributed to Francisco Ceballos); Elústiza, pages 141-43; Eslava I-1: 102-5 (attributed to Francisco Ceballos); Rubio I: 67-72.

16. *Justorum animae*

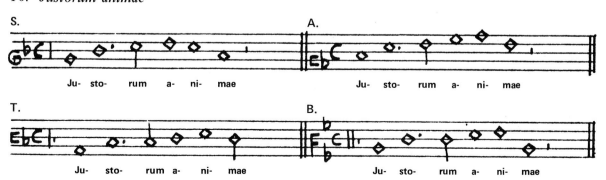

Sources   GranC LN, No. 22, anon.; GranCR 3, 69*v*-71*r,* anon.; GranCR 6, No. 10, anon.; TolC 7, 17*v*-19*r,* Ceballos.

Illustration   Folios 69*v*-70*r* of GranCR 3, Illustration 3, pages 88-89.

17. *O Doctor optime*

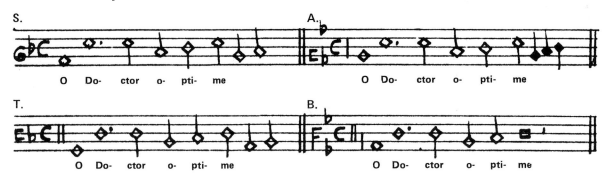

Secunda pars

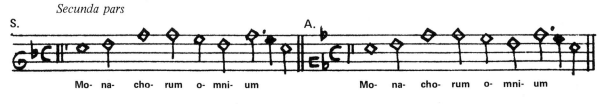

Sources   GranCR 3, 60*v*-65*r,* anon.; TolC 7, 21*v*-24*r,* Ceballos.

18. *Posuerunt super caput ejus*

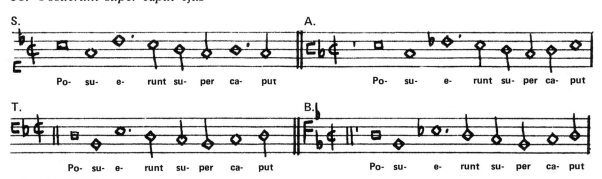

Sources   GranCR 3, 14*vr*-16*r*, anon.; Monasterio PB, Ceballos; TolC 7, 59*v*-61*r*, Ceballos; VallaP s.s., 27*v*-28*r*, Rodrigo çaballos, *in feriis XL. vel in dñca in Ramis.*

Modern Edition   Elústiza, pages 138-40; Rubio I: 181-84.

19. *Regina caeli*

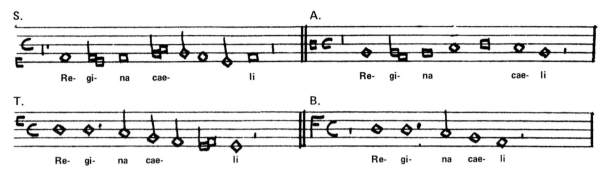

Sources   GranCR 3, 36*v*-39*r*, anon.; Monasterio PB, Ceballos; TolC 7, 6*r*-7*r*, Ceballos, incomplete.

20. *Salve Regina*

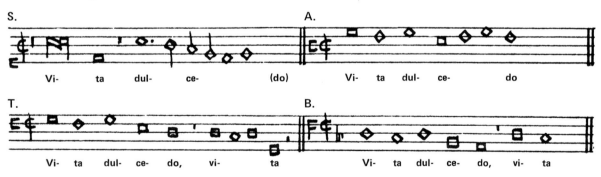

Secunda pars

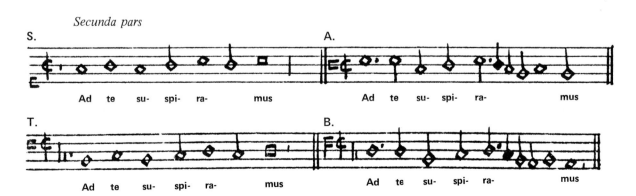

Tertia pars

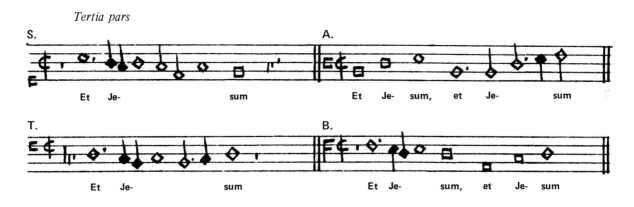

Quarta pars

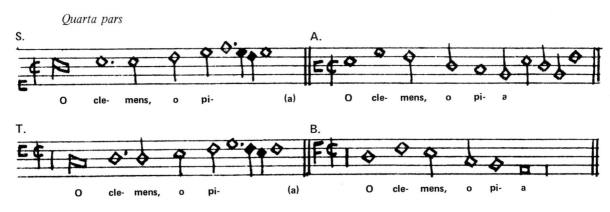

Sources BogC GFH, pages 122-25, Ceballos; SevCA 1, 21*v*-25*r*, Roderice cevallos; TolC 7, 201*v*-205*r*, Ceballos.

Illustration Folios 21*v*-22*r* of SevCA 1, Illustration 4, pages 90-91.

21. *Sancte Paule Apostole*

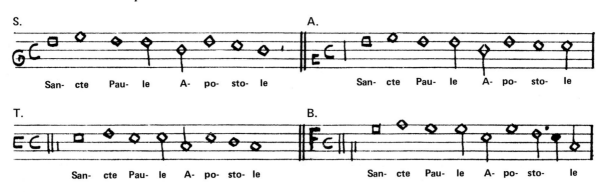

Sources GranCR 3, 67*v*-69*r*, anon.; TolC 7, 24*v*-26*r*, Ceballos.

22. *Veni Domine et noli tardare*

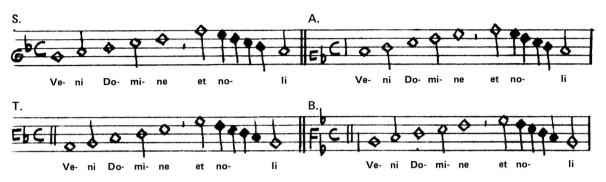

Sources   GranCR 3, 3v-6r, anon., *In Advent. Dn̄i.;*   TolC 7, 31v-34r, Ceballos.

MOTETS a 5

23. *Ad Dominum cum tribularer*

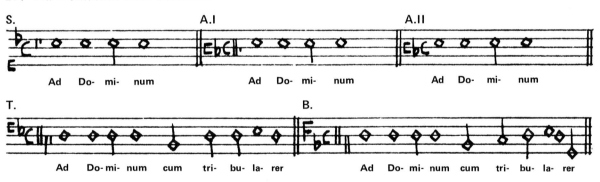

Secunda pars

Sources   GranCR 3, 115v-125r, anon.; Monasterio PB, Ceballos; TolC 7, 76v-84r, Ceballos.

24. *Ambulans Jesus*

Sources GranCR 3, *72v-75r,* anon.; TolC 7, *94v-98r,* Ceballos.

25. *Cum audisset David rex*

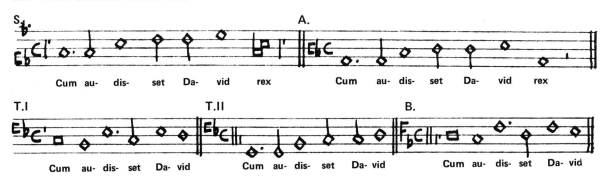

Sources GranCR 3, *128v-132r,* anon.; TolC 7, *84v-87r,* Ceballos.

Modern Edition Number 4 of Four Motets, pages 149-55.

26. *Diligite justitiam*

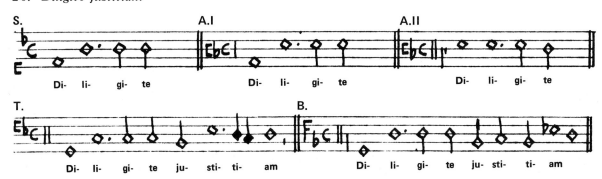

Sources GranCR 3, *125v-128r,* anon.; TolC 7, *134v-136r,* Ceballos.

Modern Edition Number 3 of Four Motets, pages 143-48.

27. *Dixit Jesus discipulis suis*

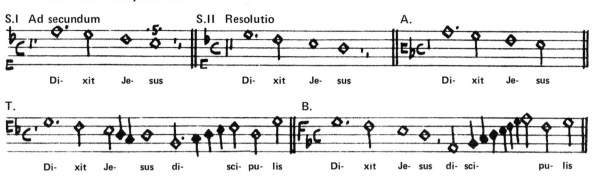

Sources   GranCR 3, 75*v*-79*r*, anon.; TolC 7, 90*v*-94*r*, Ceballos.

28. *Ecce nunc tempus acceptabile*

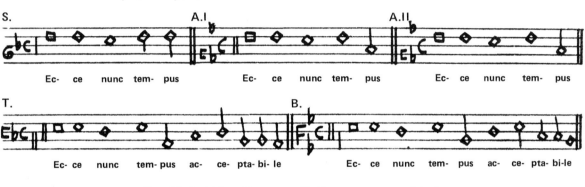

Sources   GranCR 3, 142*v*-145*r*, anon.; TolC 7, 114*v*-117*r*, Ceballos.

29. *Ecce sacerdos magnus, in fide sua*

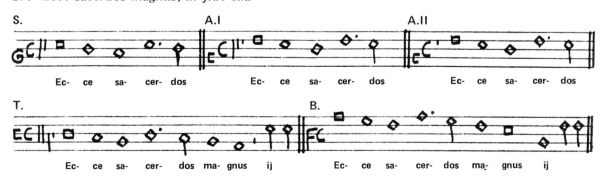

Sources   GranCR 3, 139*v*-142*r*, anon.; TolC 7, 127*v*-130*r*, Ceballos.

30. *In illo tempore: Descendens Petrus*

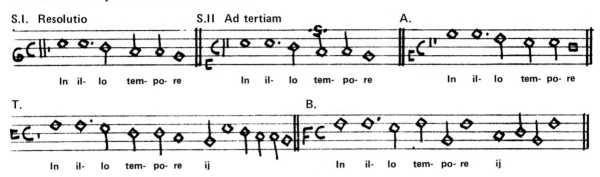

Sources   GranCR 3, 79*v*-84*r*, anon.; Monasterio PB, Ceballos; TolC 7, 98*v*-101*r*, Ceballos.

31. *In mense autem sexto*

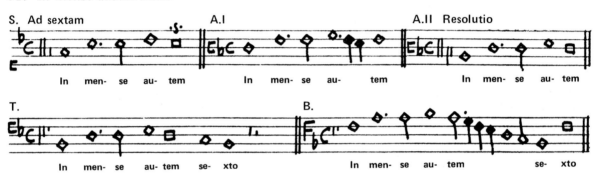

Sources   GranCR 3, 95*v*-98*r*, anon.; Monasterio PB, Ceballos; TolC 7, 66*v*-69*r*, Ceballos.

32. *Introduxit me rex*

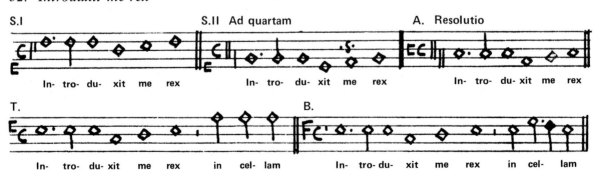

Sources   GranCR 3, 84*v*-89*r*, anon.; TolC 7, 110*v*-114*r*, Ceballos.

33. *O pretiosum et admirabile sacramentum*

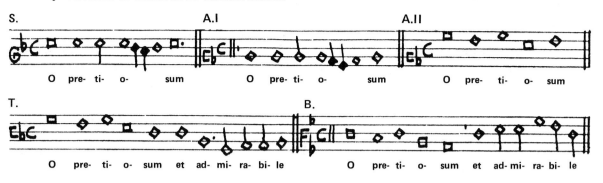

Sources   GranCR 3, 132*v*-136*r*, anon.; TolC 7, 87*v*-90*r*, Ceballos.

34. *O Virgo benedicta*

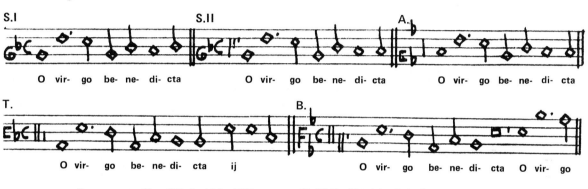

Sources   GranCR 3, 102*v*-107*r*, anon.; TolC 7, 61*v*-66*r*, Ceballos.

35. *Respicientes autem in caelum*

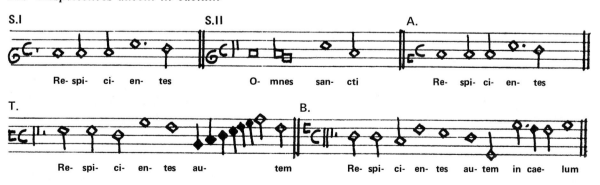

Sources   GranCR 3, 145*v*-149*r*, anon.; TolC 7, 132*v*-134*r*, Ceballos, with "Aspicientes" in lieu of "Respicientes."

Illustration   Folios 145*v*-146*r* of GranCR 3, Illustration 5, pages 92-93.

36. *Salve Sancte Francisce*

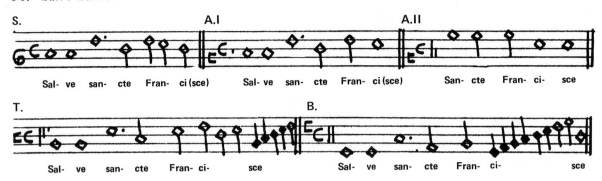

Sources   GranCR 3, 136*v*-139*r*, anon.; TolC 7, 130*v*-132*r*, Ceballos.

37. *Si quis vult post me venire*

Sources   GranCR 3, 89*v*-95*r*, anon.; TolC 7, 101*v*-106*r*, Ceballos.

38. *Spiritus Domini*

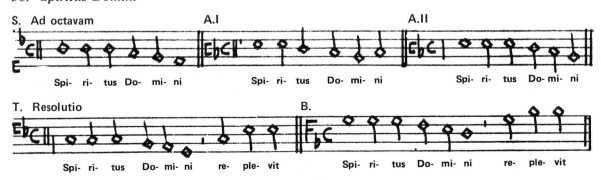

Sources   GranCR 3, 98*v*-102*r*, anon.; TolC 7, 106*v*-110*r*, Ceballos.

39. Voce mea

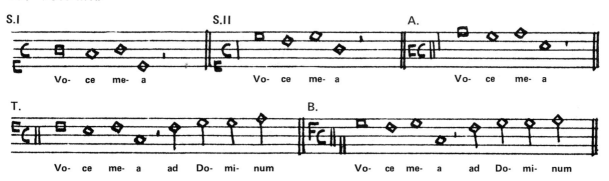

Secunda pars

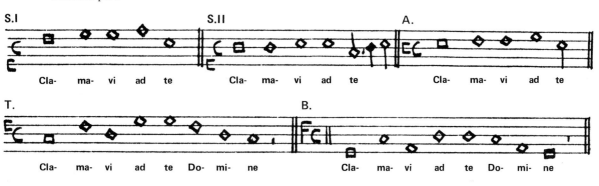

Sources   GranCR 3, 107*v*-115*r*, anon.; TolC 7, 69*v*-73*r*, Ceballos.

MASS ORDINARIES

40. Missa Simile est regnum caelorum

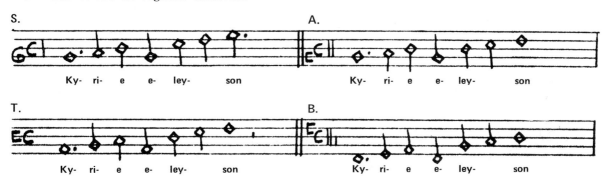

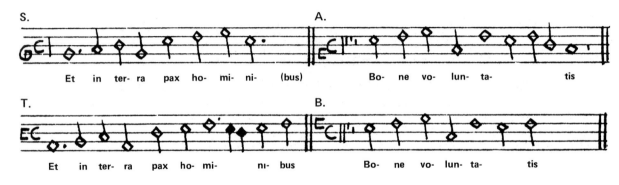

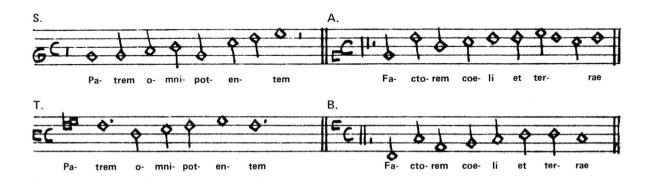

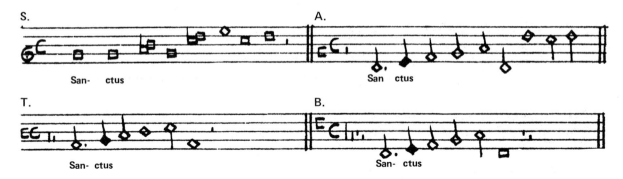

In three sections: "Sanctus . . . gloria tua," "Hosanna" and "Benedictus" (SSAT).

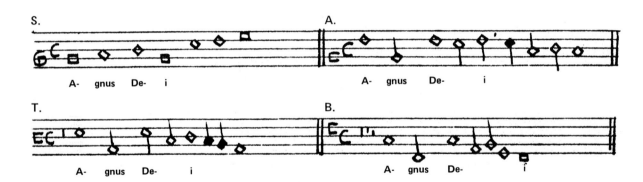

One invocation *a 4,* which concludes with "miserere nobis," and one *a 5* (SAATB, with the bass canonically derived from the tenor *subdiapente*), which concludes with "dona nobis pacem."

Sources   GuatC 1, 133*v*-152*r*, Ceballos; JaenC s.s., 58*v*-63*r*, Cevallos, *Missa a 4 en Rogaciones,* Kyrie, "Sanctus . . . gloria tua," "Agnus Dei I" only; TolC 7, 268*v*-292*r*, Ceballos.

Illustration   Folios 58*v*-59*r* of JaenC s.s., Illustration 6, pages 94-95.

41. *Missa tertii toni*

In four sections: "Sanctus," "Pleni," "Hosanna" and "Benedictus" (SAT).

Three invocations, the third of which is *a 5* (SAATB), with the bass canonically derived from the altus *subdiapason.*

Sources   AvilaC 1, pages 33-62, anon., Credo incomplete (one folio missing), Sanctus consists only of first section of the text, Agnus Dei consists only of the first invocation; AvilaC 2, pages 182-213, anon., Sanctus consists of first section somewhat rewritten so that it also accommodates the "Pleni" text, Agnus Dei as in AvilaC 1; BloomL 3, 1*v*-8*r,* anon., Sanctus incomplete, Agnus Dei missing; GuatC 1, 54*v*-71*r,* Ceballos, with shortened Sanctus and Agnus Dei; HuescaC 52, 29*v*-40*r,* Çavallos, Sanctus consists of the first two sections joined into one, Agnus Dei consists of first invocation to which an early eighteenth-century composer added an extension to which is sung the text of the third invocation; JacalP 7, pages 34-47, Saballos, Kyrie and Gloria only; PampC, anon.(?); SantiC 3, 45*v*-62*r,* anon.(?); SaraP 8, 25*v*-33*r,* Çavallos, Sanctus consists only of the first section, Agnus Dei only of the first invocation; Tol 1696, Ceballos(?); TolC 7, 292*v*-313*r* Ceballos, *sine nomine,* only source to contain complete, original version.

Illustrations   Folios 292*v*-293*r* of TolC 7, pages 36-37 of JacalP 7, 4*v*-5*r* of BloomL 3, 59*v*-60*r* of of AvilaC 1 and 39*v*-40*r* of HuescaC 52, Illustrations 7-11, pages 96-105.

42. *Missa Veni Domine*

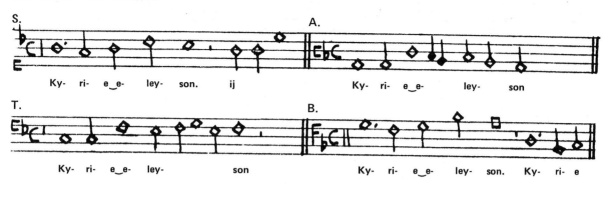

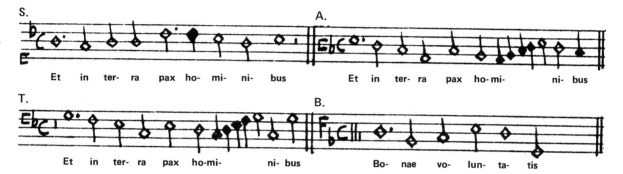

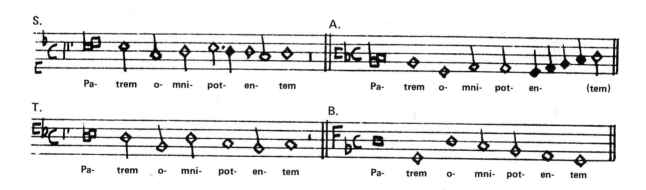

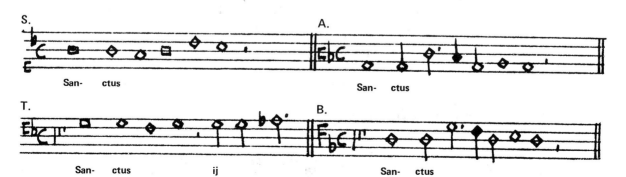

In four sections: "Sanctus," "Pleni" (SAT), "Hosanna" and "Benedictus."

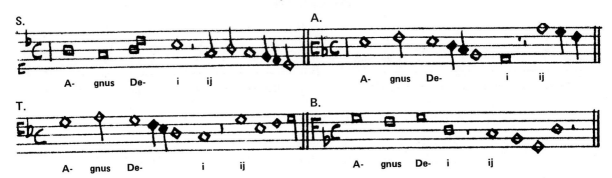

One invocation *a 4*, which concludes with "miserere nobis," and one *a 5* (SAATB, with the tenor derived from the superius *subdiapason*), which concludes with "dona nobis pacem."

Sources   TolC 7, 315*v*-336*r*, Ceballos.

Illustrations   Folios 317*v*-318*r* and 332*v*-333*r* of TolC 7, Illustrations 12-13, pages 106-9.

VESPERS PSALMS

43. Dixit Dominus (Ps. 109).   Tone 1

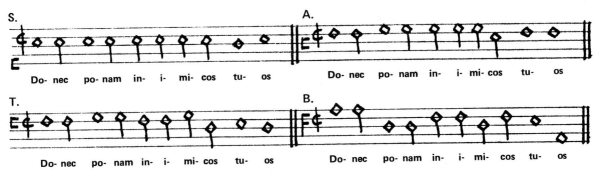

Verses 2, 4, 6, 8, 10 (Sicut erat).

Sources   BogC GFH, pages 52-55, R.º Çaballos; PuebC VI, 3*v*-5*r*, anon., verse 9 (Gloria Patri) instead of verse 10 (Sicut erat); PuebC XIX, [i]*v*-1*v*, anon., verses 2, 4 and S and T of 6, 8 only, textless; VilViçB 8, 24*v*-29*r*, Cevallos.

Illustration   Folios 3*v*-4*r* of PuebC VI, Illustration 14, pages 110-11.

44. Dixit Dominus (Ps. 109).   Tone 3

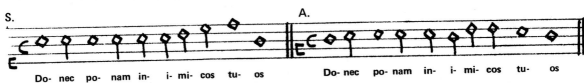

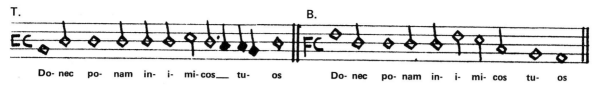

Do- nec po- nam in- i- mi-cos__ tu- os   Do- nec po- nam in- i- mi-cos tu- os

Verses 2, 4, 6, 8, 10 (Sicut erat).

Sources   BogC Apost, No. 1, Cevallos; BogC GFH, pages 56-59, Ceballos, *muy abreviado para dias menos solesmnes;* BogC Virg, No. 1, Ceballos; PuebC VI, 21*v*-23*r*, anon.

45a. *Dixit Dominus* (Ps. 109). Tone 4

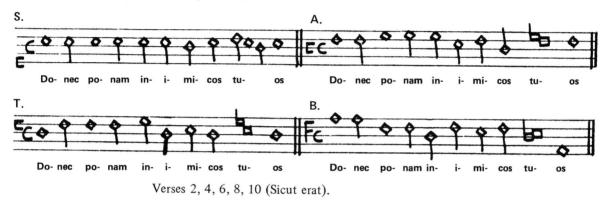

Verses 2, 4, 6, 8, 10 (Sicut erat).

Sources   GranC 4, 13*v*-16*r*, anon.; GranC 4, 16*v*-19*r*, anon., with verse 9 (Gloria Patri) instead of verse 10 (Sicut erat); GranCR 4, 18*v*-21*r*, anon.; PuebC VI, 23*v*-25*r*, anon.; SegC 4, 21*v*-23*r*, Zavallos.

45b. *Dixit Dominus* (Ps. 109). Tone 4

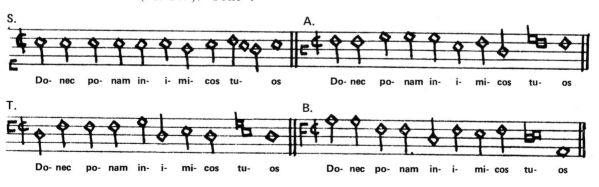

Variant of 45a.

Verses 2, 4, 6, 8, 10 (Sicut erat).

Sources   BogC GFH, pages 94-97, Ceballos, *abreviado.*

46a. *Dixit Dominus* (Ps. 109). Tone 6

Identified from relationship with 46b.

Verses 2, 4, 6, 8, 10 (Sicut erat).

Sources GranC 4, 19*v*-22*r,* anon.; GranCR 4, 3*v*-6*r,* anon., verse 9 (Gloria Patri) instead of verse 10 (Sicut erat); GranCR 4, 9*v*-12*r,* anon.; PuebC VI, 22*v*-24*r,* anon.

Illustration Folios 9*v*-10*r* of GranCR 4, Illustration 15, pages 112-13.

46b. *Dixit Dominus* (Ps. 109). Tone 6

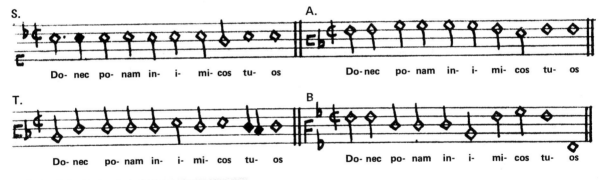

Variant of 46a.

Verses 2, 4, 6, 8, 10 (Sicut erat).

Sources BogC GFH, pages 98-101, Cevallos, *abreviado.*

Illustration Pages 98-99 of BogC GFH, Illustration 16, pages 114-15.

47. *Confitebor tibi* (Ps. 110). Tone 7

Verses 2, 4, 6, 8, 10, 12 (Sicut erat).

Sources   BogC Apost, No. 2, Cevallos; BogC GFH, pages 60-63, Çaballos, *abreviado;* PuebC XIX, 43*v*-45*r*, erroneously attributed to Guerrero, textless, verse 10 lacking; VilViçB 8, 29*v*-35*r*, Cevallos.

NB: The music for verses 8 and 10 in VilViçB 8 differs from that which is given for these two verses in the three New World sources. None of the music is that which Guerrero provides for his setting of *Confitebor tibi* in tone 7 in his *Liber vesperarum* of 1584.

48. *Laudate pueri* (Ps. 112). Tone 8

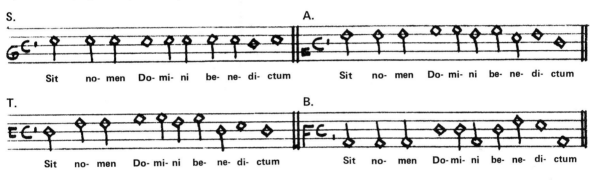

Verses 2, 4, 6, 8, 10 (Sicut erat).

Source   VilViçB 8, 40*v*-45*r*, Cevallos.

49. *In convertendo* (Ps. 125). Tone 3

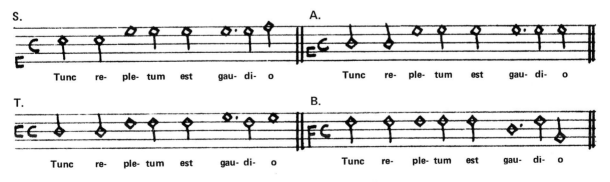

Verses 2, 4, 6, 8, 10 (Sicut erat).

Sources   PuebC VI, 98*v*-100*r*, anon.; VilViçB 8, 89*v*-93*r*, Cevallos.

50. *Lauda Jerusalem* (Ps. 147). Tone 8

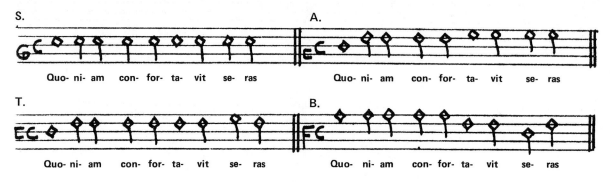

Verses 2, 4, 6, 8, 10 (Gloria Patri).

Sources	GranC 4, 91*v*-93*r*, anon.; PuebC VI, 104*v*-106*r*, anon.; SegC 4, 52*v*-54*r*, Çavallos; VilViçB 8, 56*v*-61*r*, Cevallos.
Illustration	Folios 52*v*-53*r* of SegC 4, Illustration 17, pages 116-17.

VESPERS HYMNS

51. *Aurea luce*

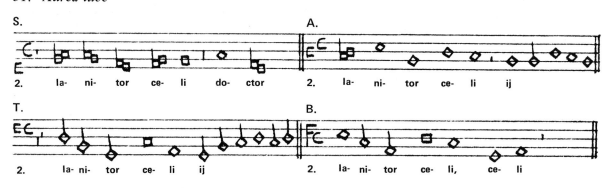

Sources	GuadM 1, 48*v*-50*r*, çavallos, *In festo apostolorum petri et pauli.*
Illustration	Folios 48*v*-49*r* of GuadM 1, Illustration 18, pages 118-19.

52. *Ave maris stella*

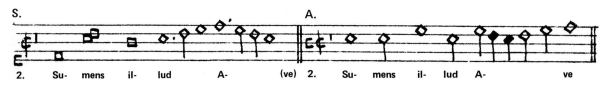

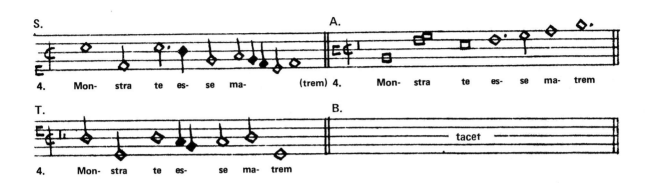

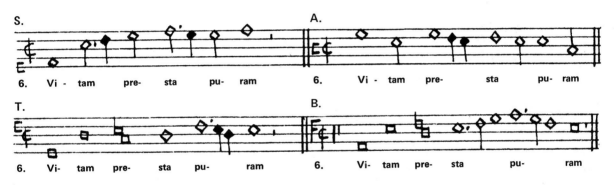

Sources   GranC 5, 22*v*-24*r*, anon., *In festivitatibus B. M.*, music for strophe 2 only with text of strophe 5 ("Virgo singularis"); VilViçB 8, 93*v*-99*r*, Cevallos.

Illustration   Folios 93*v*-94*r* of VilViçB 8, Illustration 19, pages 120-21.

53. *Exsultet caelum*

S.

A.

4. Quo- rum pre- ce- pto sub- di- tur

4. Quo- rum pre- ce- pto sub- di- tur

T.

B.

4. Quo- rum pre- ce- pto sub- di- tur

tacet

Source   VilViçB 8, 109*v*-112*r*, Cevallos.

54. *Hostis Herodes impie*

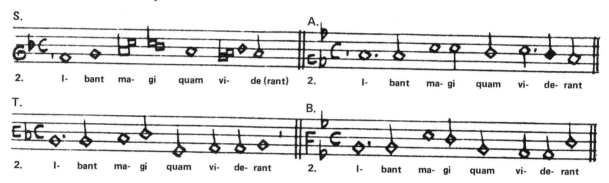

S.

A.

2. I- bant ma- gi quam vi- de (rant)

2. I- bant ma- gi quam vi- de- rant

T.

B.

2. I- bant ma- gi quam vi- de- rant

2. I- bant ma- gi quam vi- de- rant

Sources   GranC 5, 15*v*-16*r*, anon., with text of strophe 2 ("Illustre quidam") of *Quicumque Christum quaeritis, In festo Transfigurationis Dñi nostri Iesu Xpti;* GranCR 4, 130*v*-132*r*, anon., with same text as in GranC 5; GuadM 1, 72*v*-74*r*, çavallos, *in epiphania Dñi.,* music for strophe 2 only, as given above.

55. *Pange lingua*

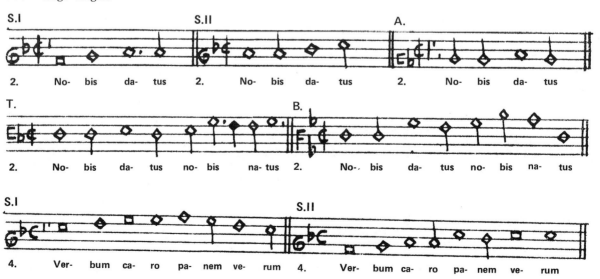

S.I

S.II

A.

2. No- bis da- tus

2. No- bis da- tus

2. No- bis da- tus

T.

B.

2. No- bis da- tus no- bis na- tus

2. No- bis da- tus no- bis na- tus

S.I

S.II

4. Ver- bum ca- ro pa- nem ve- rum

4. Ver- bum ca- ro pa- nem ve- rum

S.III   T.

4.   Ver- bum ca- ro pa- nem ve- rum   4.   Ver- bum ca- ro pa- nem ve- rum

Sources   GuadM 1, 86*v*-88*r*, Çavallos, *In festo Corporis Christi*, music and text of strophe 4 only; PuebC XIX, 63*v*-65*r*, Ceballos, music and textual incipit of strophe 2, and 59*v*-60*r*, Ceballos, music and textual incipit of strophe 4; SaraP 34, 21*r*-21*v*, çavallos, S. I only of strophe 4; VilViçB 8, 105*v*-109*r*, Cevallos, with strophe 2 *a 4*, strophe 4 as given above.

56. Vexilla Regis

S.   A.

2.   Quo vul- ne- ra- tus in- su- per   2.   Quo vul- ne- ra- tus in- su- per

T.   B.

2.   Quo vul- ne- ra- tus in- su- (per)   2.   Quo vul- ne- ra- tus in- su- per

S.I   S.II

4.   Ar- bor de- co- ra- ful- gi- (da)   4.   Ar- bor de- co- ra ful- gi- da

A.   T.

4.   Ar- bor de- co- ra- ful- gi- da   4.   Ar- bor de- co- ra ful- gi- da

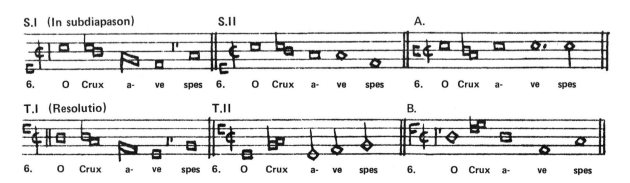

S.I (In subdiapason)   S.II   A.

6.   O Crux a- ve spes   6.   O Crux a- ve spes   6.   O Crux a- ve spes

T.I (Resolutio)   T.II   B.

6.   O Crux a- ve spes   6.   O Crux a- ve spes   6.   O Crux a- ve spes

Sources   PuebC I, 60v-62r, anon., music of strophe 2 above but with text of strophe 1 plus additional part (S. II) probably not by Ceballos; PuebC II, A:18v-21r, anon., music of strophes 2 and 4 as above but with text of strophes 1 and 3; PuebC II, A:22v-24r, music of strophe 6 above but with doxological strophe and erroneously attributed to Guerrero; PuebC II, A:38v-39v, anon., music of strophe 2 above but with text of strophe 1 plus the additional part found in PuebC 1, incomplete; VilViçB 8, 99v-105r, Cevallos, strophes 2, 4, 6 as given above.

MAGNIFICAT SETTINGS

57. *Magnificat.*   Tone 1

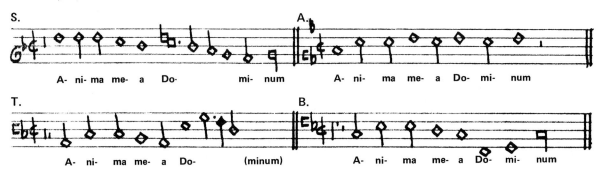

Verses 1, 3, 5 (SAT), 7, 9, 11.

Sources   BogC A, 105v-106v and 108r-108v, cevallos, verses 5, 7, 9 and 11 incomplete; BogC C, pages 1-8, Zevallos; BogC Virg, No. 6, Ceballos, verse 5 missing.

Illustration   Pages 1-2 of BogC C in Perdomo, opposite page 448.

58. *Magnificat.*   Tone 2

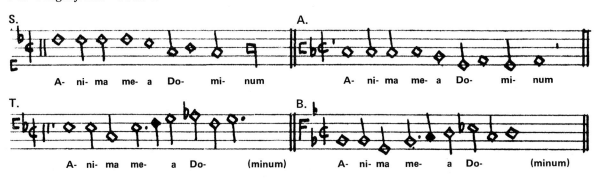

Verses 1, 3, 5 (SAT), 7, 9, 11.

Sources   BogC A, 111r-112v, cevallos, verses 1, 3 and 11 missing, verses 5 and 9 incomplete; BogC C, pages 9-18, Zevallos; GuadM 1, 89v-91r and 92v-95r, Çavallos, with an alternate setting of verse 7 (SAT) by Ribera on 91v-92r.

59. *Magnificat.* Tone 3

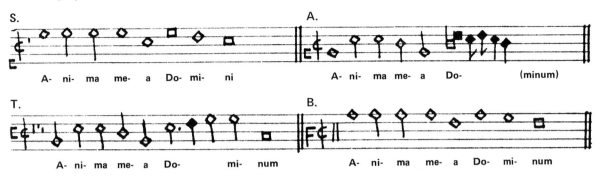

Verses 1, 3, 5 (SAT), 7, 9, 11.

Sources   BogC A, 115r-115v and 117r-118*bisr*, cevallos, only verses 9 and 11 complete; BogC C, pages 19-28, Zevallos.

60. *Magnificat.* Tone 4

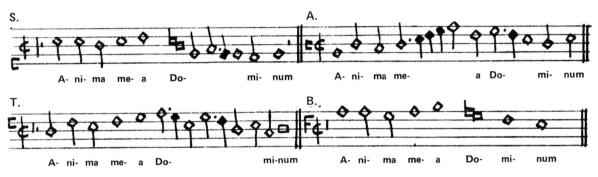

Verses 1, 3, 5 (SAT), 7, 9, 11.

Sources   BogC A, 118*bisr*-122r, cevallos; BogC B, three unnumbered pages containing A and B of verse 9 and SATB of verse 11, (Cevallos); BogC C, pages 29-38, Zevallos.

Illustration   Pages 29-30 of BogC C, Illustration 20, pages 122-23.

61. *Magnificat.* Tone 5

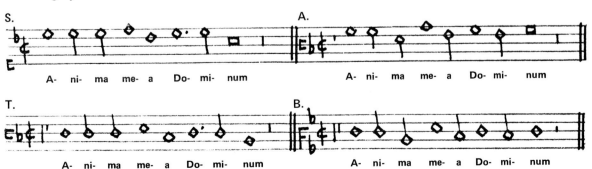

Verses 1, 3, 5 (SAT), 7, 9, 11.

Sources   BogC A, 122*v*-127*r*, cevallos; BogC Apost, No. 6, Ceballos; BogC B, ten unnumbered pages, Ceballos; BogC C, pages 39-48, Zevallos.

62. *Magnificat*. Tone 6

Verses 1, 3, 5 (SAT), 7, 9, 11.

Sources   BogC A, 127*v*-131*r*, cevallos; BogC B, one unnumbered page with S and T of verses 1 and 3, Ceballos; BogC C, pages 49-58, Zevallos.

63. *Magnificat*. Tone 7

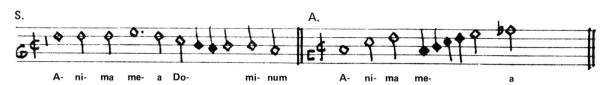

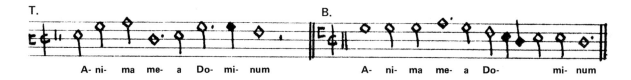

Verses 1, 3, 5 (SAT), 7, 9, 11.

Sources   BogC A, 131*v*-134*v*, cevallos, A and B of verse 11 missing; BogC C, pages 59-68, Zevallos.

Illustration   Folios 131*v*-132*r* of BogC A, Illustration 21, pages 124-25.

64. *Magnificat*. Tone 8

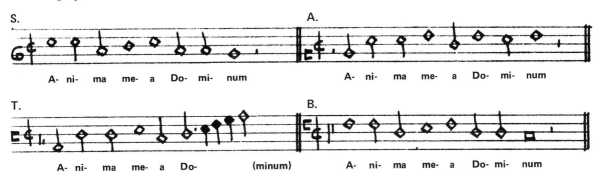

S. A- ni- ma me- a Do- mi- num
A. A- ni- ma me- a Do- mi- num
T. A- ni- ma me- a Do- (minum)
B. A- ni- ma me- a Do- mi- num

Verses 1, 3, 5 (SAT), 7, 9, 11.

Sources   BogC A, 135*bis*r-138r, cevallos, S and T of verse 1 missing; BogC C, pages 69-78, Zevallos.

65. *Magnificat*. Tone 6

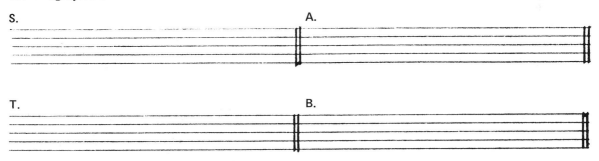

S.   A.

T.   B.

Verses 2, 4, 6, 8, 10, 12 (?).

Source   GuatC 2, B:132*v*-138r, Ceballos. (See footnote 40, page 30.)

MUSIC FOR COMPLINE

66. *Qui habitat in adjutorio Altissimi* (Psalm 90)

S. Qui ha- bi- tat in ad- ju- to- ri- o
A. Qui ha- bi- tat in ad- ju- to- ri- o
T. Qui ha- bi- tat in ad- ju- to- ri- o
B. Qui ha- bi- tat in ad- ju- to- ri- o

Verses 1, 3, 5, 7 (two settings), 9, 11, 13, 15 (two settings, the second *sençillo*), 17 (Gloria Patri).

Source   NYorkHS 380/870, 109*v*-117*r*, De Zaballos.

67. *Ecce nunc benedicite* (Psalm 133)

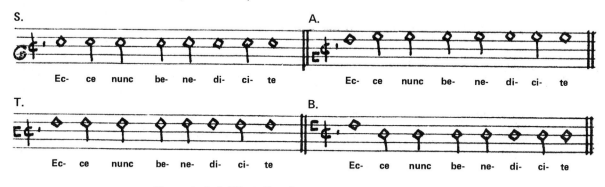

Verses 1, 3, 5 (Gloria Patri).

Source   NYorkHS 380/870, 116*v*-118*r*, Zaballos.

68. *In manus tuas* (Responsorium breve)

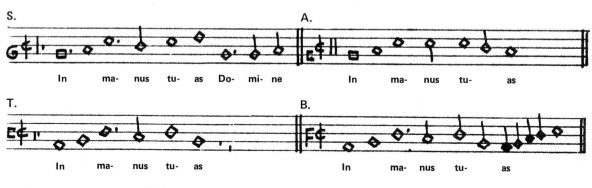

Entire text set.

Source   NYorkHS 380/870, 119*bis*v-121*r*, Zaballos.

69. *Custodi nos, Domine* (Versicle)

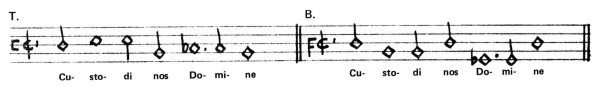

Source NYorkHS 380/870, 121*v*-122*r*, Zaballos.

70. *Nunc dimittis* (Canticle of Zachary)

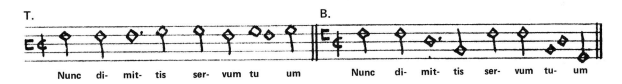

Verses 1, 3 (two settings, the second *sençillo*), 5 (Gloria Patri).

Source NYorkHS 380/870, 118*v*-119*bisr*, Zaballos.

Illustration Folio 119*r* of NYorkHS 380/870 in Penney, page 392.

DISMISSAL VERSICLES-RESPONSES

71. *Benedicamus Domino*

Source GuadM I, 103*v*-104*r*, çavallos.

72. *Deo dicamus gratias*

Source   SevCA 1, 95*v*-96*r*, Roderice cevallos.

SECULAR WORKS

73. *Amargas oras*

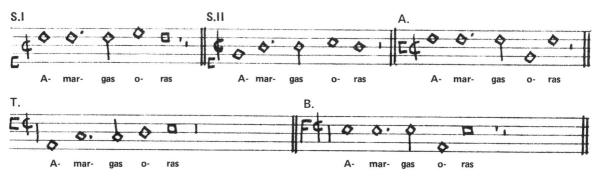

Source   MadBM 13230, 10*v*-11*r*, Cevallos.

Modern Edition   Querol I: 22-25.

74. *Dime manso viento*

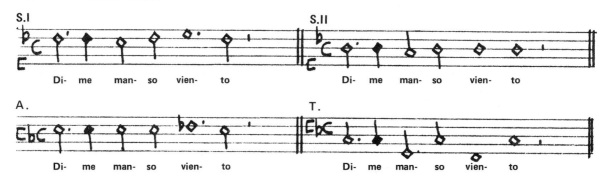

Sources	MadBM 13230, 135*v*-136*r,* anon.; PuebC XIX, 145*v*-146*r,* anon., text incipits only; VallaC 17, 20*v*-21*r,* anon., altus only, textless; Daza, 93*r*-94*r,* Caballos (Zaballos in index), *villanesca.*
Modern Edition	Querol II: 75-77; Morphy, pages 244-45.
Illustration	Folios 145*v*-146*r,* of PuebC XIX, Illustration 22, pages 126-27.

75. *Duro mal, terrible llanto*

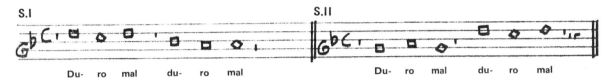

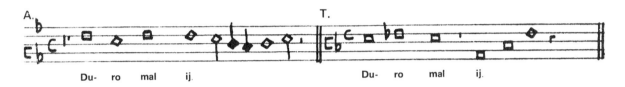

Sources	MadBM 13230, 134*v*-135*r,* anon.; Daza, 91*v*-93*r,* Caballos (Zaballos in index), *villanesca.*
Modern Edition	Querol II: 72-74.

76. *Ojos hermosos*

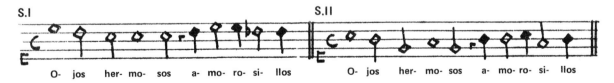

Source	MadBM 13230, 49*v*-50*r, de Cevallos y la 4ª boz de varrio nue̮vo.*
Modern Edition	Querol I: 89-90.

77. *Pues ya las claras fuentes*

Sources	Daza, 84r-85r, Zaballos, *villanesca.*
Modern Edition	Morphy, pages 251-52.

78. *Quan bien aventurado*

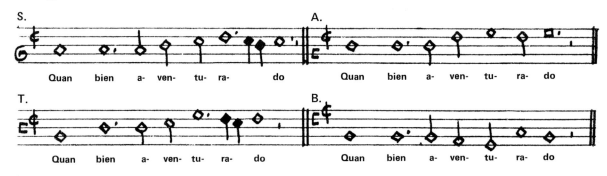

Sources	MadBM 13230, 129v-130r, Cevallos; VallaC 17, 5v-6r, Cevallos, tenor only; Daza, 81v-83r, anon., *cancion.*
Modern Edition	Querol II: 54-57; Trend, pages 241-43, incomplete.

79. *Rosales, mirtos, plátanos*

Sources   MadBM 13230, 71*v*-72*r,* anon.; MadBM 13230, 94*v,* R.º Cevallos, S. I and T only; VallaC 17, 28*v*-29*r,* anon., altus only, textless.

Modern Edition   Querol I: 125-27.

DUBIOUS WORKS

Gaude Dei genitrix

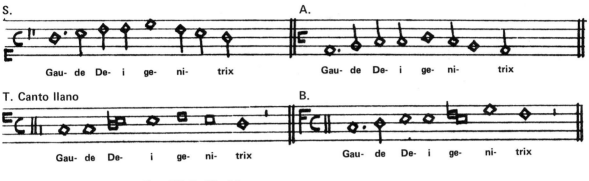

Source   GranCR 3, 50*v*-54*r,* anon.

Nine "Fabordones"

1º

2º

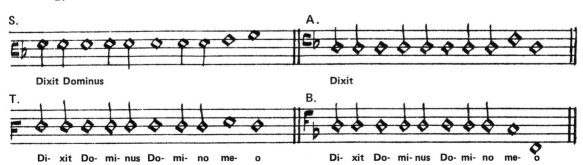

7º

8º

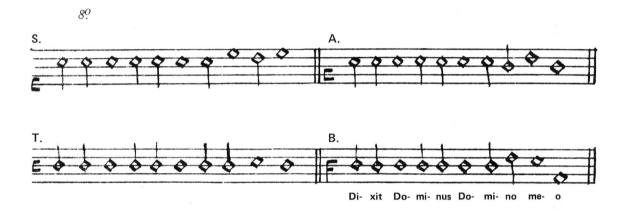

8º *irregular*

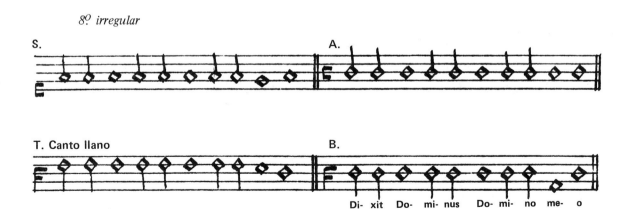

Source   MontsB 750, 36*v*-41*r*, anon., *Fabordones con el canto llano. A 4. Como se cantan en s. lorencio. Pueden yr por qualquier psalmo y son muy acomodados.*

Modern Edition   Pedrell VI: 20-22, but not based on MontsB 750; see pages 32-33, above.

THE EXTANT MUSIC OF

RODRIGO DE CEBALLOS
AND ITS SOURCES
Thematic Incipits   Illustrations   Four Motets

Illustration 1
Item No. 5
Granada. Capilla Real, Archivo Capitular. Ms. 3, folios 6v-7r.
Beginning of the motet *Ductus est Jesus.*

U ctus est Jesus in dese r tum in dese

tū a spi ri tu ut tentaretur a dia bo

lo, et cū jeiuņa set quadragīta di

e bus, et quadragīta noctib, postea esu rijt

Et accedēs tētator dixit e i

T tentare tur á di a bo lo a di

a bolo, ut tentaretur a di a bo lo

quadraginta di e bu s, et quadraginta noctibus,

poste a e furi jt. Et acce dens tēta

tor,

Illustration 2
Item No. 8
Valladolid.
Parroquia de Santiago.
Manuscript without number
(Diego Sánchez codex),
folios 33*v*-34*r*.

Beginning of the motet
*Erat Jesus ejiciens
daemonium*.

Illustration 3
Item No. 16
Granada. Capilla Real,
Archivo Capitular.
Ms. 3, folios 69*v*-70*r*.
Beginning of the motet
Justorum animae.

Us to rum ani mæ ij

Justoruma ni mæ ij

in manu De i sunt ij

in manu de i sunt, et non tanget illos

et non tanget

Us to rum ani mæ ij

in ma nu De i sunt ij

ij et non tanget

illos.

Illustration 4
Item No. 20
Seville. Catedral,
Archivo Capitular.
Ms. 1, folios 21*v*-22*r*.
Beginning of the
Marian antiphon
Salve Regina.

Illustration 5
Item No. 35
Granada. Capilla Real,
Archivo Capitular.
Ms. 3, folios 145*v*-146*r*.
Beginning of the motet
Respicientes.

O̲mnes sancti et sā
cte Dei. O rate pro nobis.

E̲spicientes autē in celū, san
cti martires. Sāctimartires,di xe runt, Di

xerunt, Benedicimus te, Deus noster, qui

E̲spicientes autem

in ce lum, Sancti mar ti res Dixe

runt, Benedicimus,

Illustration 6
Item No. 40
Jaen. Catedral, Archivo Capitular. Manuscript without number, folios 58*v*-59*r*.
"Kyrie I" and "Christe" of the Kyrie of *Missa Simile est regnum caelorum.*

Illustration 7
Item No. 41
Toledo. Catedral,
Archivo y Biblioteca
Capitulares.
Ms. Mus. B. 7,
folios 292*v*-293*r*.

"Kyrie I" and
"Christe" of the
Kyrie of
Missa tertii toni.

96

97

Illustration 8
Item No. 41

Jacaltenango.
Iglesia Parroquial
de Santa Eulalia,
Archivo Musical.
Ms. 7, pages 36-37.

Beginning of the
Gloria of
Missa tertii toni.

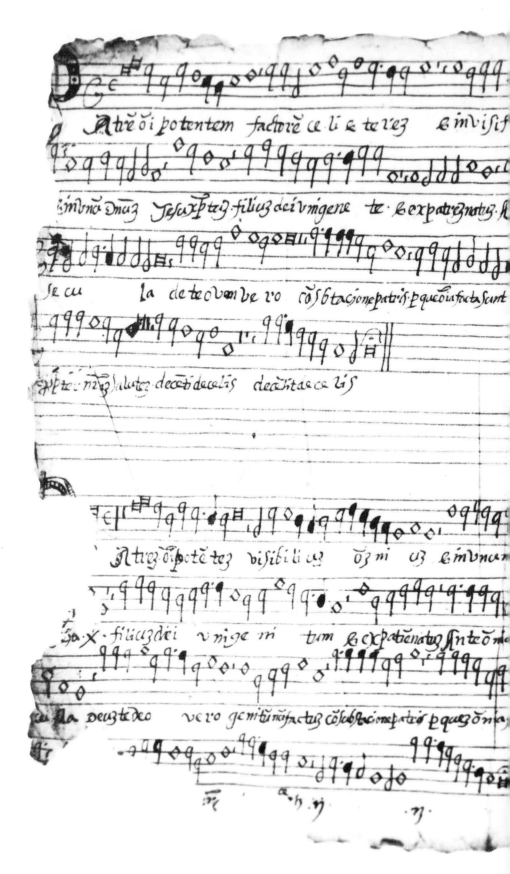

Illustration 9
Item No. 41
Bloomington.
Indiana University,
Lilly Library. Latin
American Manuscripts,
Guatemala.
Mus. Ms. 3, folios 4*v*-5*r*.

Beginning of the
Credo of
Missa tertii toni.

Ab̃ m̃ ōi poten̄   factorem se liōteres: ē inuisifili um: ē

ā d̃omin̄ Jesu christe filiu̅ s̃ deiunigen̄ite   e xp̄a triānatu̅s

ōia sc̄ula de b̃ue ro genitu̅s factu̅s cōsubtacionē patris per quem̄ ōi sac

qui ppter nos ommis   e. ppter n̄ra s̄a luters clec̃ātit

ul iũ s ij̃

Ntrē zōm potētez factorē m celieterr̃ c̃ e m̃ b̃nu̅ Domin̄us

e ju xp̄e filitum dei v̄mige ni   tu̅s Ante ōm secu la lum̃e

n̄i ne d̃ōm̄ie ro de t un̄e   ro cōsubtacion̄

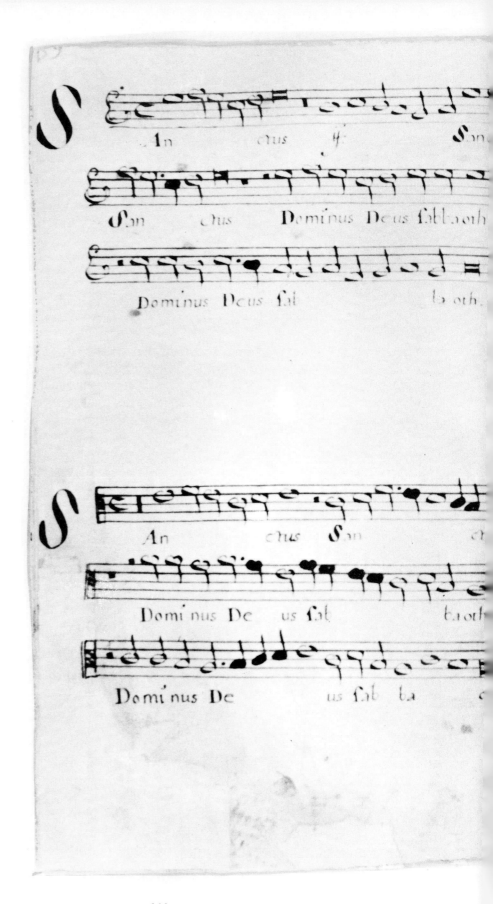

Illustration 10
Item No. 41

Avila. Catedral,
Archivo Capitular.
Ms. 1, folios 59*v*-60*r*.

Beginning of the
Sanctus of
Missa tertii toni.

San   An   ctus   ij

San   ctus   Dominus Deus Sabbaoth

Dominus Deus   Dominus Deus Sabba oth.

An   ctus   ij   San

ctus   Dominus De us   sab   ba oth

Domi nus De us   sab   ba oth.

Illustration 11
Item No. 41

Huesca. Catedral,
Archivo Capitular.
Ms. 52, folios 39*v*-40*r*.

Beginning of the
Agnus Dei of
Missa tertii toni.

The music through the words
". . . miserere nobis." is by
Ceballos; the continuation is
by an anonymous composer of
the early eighteenth century
and replaces the five-part
setting which Ceballos provided
for the invocation ending
". . . dona nobis pacem."

Illustration 12
Item No. 42
Toledo. Catedral,
Archivo y Biblioteca
Capitulares.
Ms. Mus. B. 7,
folios 317*v*-318*r*.
Beginning of the
Gloria of
Missa Veni Domine.

107

Illustration 13
Item No. 42
Toledo. Catedral, Archivo y Biblioteca Capitulares.
Ms. Mus. B. 7, folios 332*v*-333*r*.
"Benedictus" of the Sanctus of
Missa Veni Domine.

Ve ni domine et noli tardare

Ve ni domine Et noli tardare.

Be ne dictus qui venit

Be nedict qui venit

In no mine domi

nr dni domi ni In nomi ne dni in

ne mine ij domini

Illustration 14
Item No. 43
Puebla. Catedral,
Archivo Musical.
Libro de coro VI,
folios 3*v*-4*r*.
Verses 2, 4 and 6
of the psalm
Dixit Dominus, tone 1.

Onec ponam ini mi cos tuos, scabellum pedum tuo

Tecum principium in di e virtutis tu e, in splendoribus sanctoʒ

ex vte ro ante lu ci fe rum genu i te.

Domi nus a dextris tu is, confregit in die irę suę re ges.

Onec ponam inimicos tuos, scabellum pedum tuo

Tecum principium in die vir tu tis tu ę, in splendoribus sanctoʒ ex vte

ro ante lu ci fe rum genui te genu i te.

Domi nus a dextris tuis confregit in die i tę suę re

ges,

Illustration 15
Item No. 46a
Granada. Capilla Real,
Archivo Capitular.
Ms. 4, folios 9*v*-10*r*.
Verses 2 and 4
of the psalm
Dixit Dominus, tone 6.

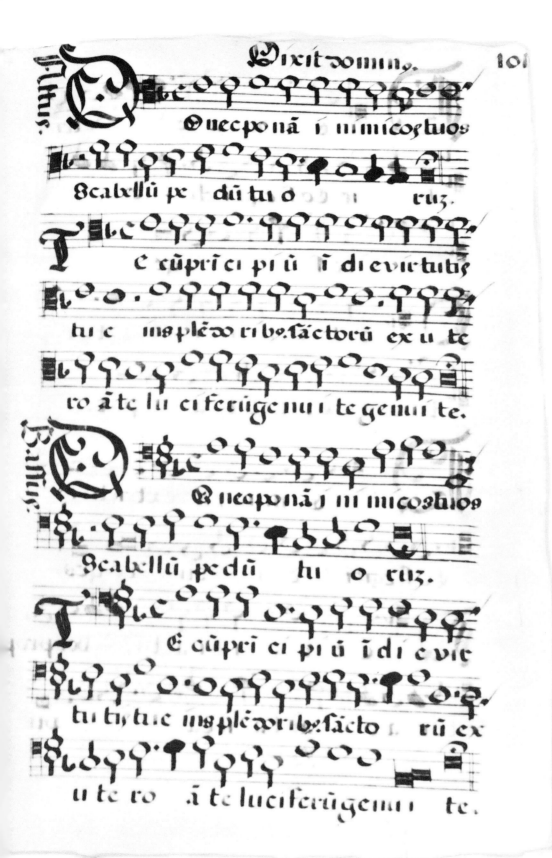

Illustration 16
Item No. 46b
Bogotá. Catedral,
Archivo Musical.
Gutierre Fernández
Hidalgo codex, pages 98-99.

Verses 2, 4 and 6
of the psalm
Dixit Dominus,
tone 6, *abreviado*.

Illustration 17
Item No. 50

Segovia. Catedral,
Archivo Capitular.
Ms. 4, folios 52*v*-53*r*.

Verses 2 and 4
of the psalm
Lauda Jerusalem, tone 8.

Illustration 18
Item No. 51

Guadalupe. Real
Monasterio de Santa María,
Archivo, Ms. 1,
folios 48*v*-49*r*.

Beginning of
strophe 2 of the
hymn *Aurea luce*.

49.

119

Illustration 19
Item No. 52
Vila Viçosa. Casa de Braganza, Museu-Biblioteca. Ms. 8, folios 93*v*-94*r*.
Beginning of strophe 2 of the hymn *Ave maris stella*.

S

umens illud A ve

gabri e lis o re

fundanos in pa

S

umens illud Ave

gabrie lis o re

fundanos in

Illustration 20
Item No. 60
Bogotá. Catedral,
Archivo Musical.
Manuscript without number
copied *c.* 1800
(BogC C), pages 29-30.
Verses 1 and 3 of the
Magnificat, tone 4.

Anima mea a Do — minum.ij

Quia respexit humilitatem ancille su   & ecce enim   ecce e-

nium cohocbea tam me i   cent omnes ge nera-

tio   nes ij

Quarto Tono

Magnificat

Anima mea Dominum ij

Quia respexit humilitatem ancille sue ecce enim ij   ex hoc beatam

me   dicent ij   omnes generationes ij

ij   genera tio- nes

Illustration 21
Item No. 63
Bogotá. Catedral,
Archivo Musical. Manuscript
without number copied
c. 1584-1586 (BogC A),
folios 131*v*-132*r*.
Verses 1 and 3 of the
Magnificat, tone 7.

nima mea Domi   num   ij.

Quia respexit humilitatem   ij.   ancillæ su—

E   ij.   ecce enim   ex hoc beatam me

dicunt   omnes generationes.   ij.

ij.

Magni   ficad

nima mea Dominum   dominum

Quia respexit humilitatem   ij.   ancillæ su—

ç ecce enim   ex hoc beatam   ij.   me dicent   omnes generati—

nes   ij.

Illustration 22
Item No. 74
Puebla. Catedral,
Archivo Musical.
Libro de coro XIX,
folios 145*v*-146*r*.
Dime manso viento.

Dime mango biento.

THE EXTANT MUSIC O

RODRIGO DE CEBALLOS
AND ITS SOURCES

Thematic Incipits   Illustrations   Four Motets

FOUR MOTETS

1. *Clamabat autem mulier Chananaea*

131

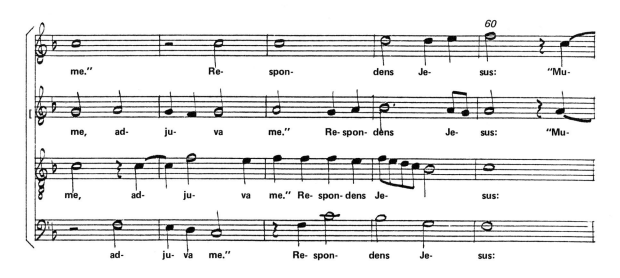

2. *Adversum me susurrabant*

is, et re- tri- bu- am e- is, et re- tri-
et re- tri- bu- am e- is, et re- tri- bu- am
re- tri- bu- am, et re- tri- bu- am e- is, re- tri- bu- am___
bu- am e- is, et re- tri- bu-

bu- am e- is.
e- is.
e- is.
- am e- is.

3. *Diligite justitiam*

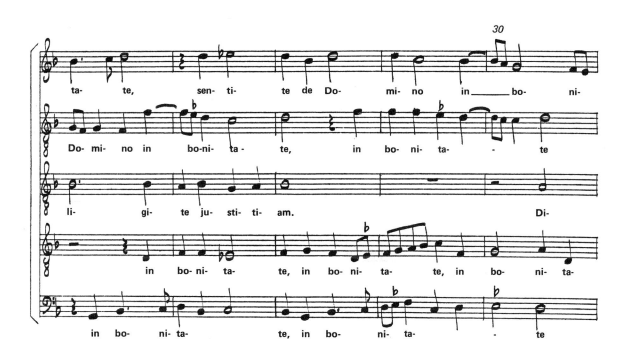

4. *Cum audisset autem David rex*